A MEDIUM'S STORY

TRUE PARANORMAL ADVENTURES

Title: *A Medium's Story – True Paranormal Adventures*
Author: Kerrie Erwin
Copyright © 2024 Kerrie Erwin
Published in 2024 by Kerrie Erwin
Contact: www.pureview.com.au
www.facebook.com/KerrieErwinPublicFigure
www.instagram.com/mediumkerrieerwin

PRINT ISBN: 9781763606500
EPUB ISBN: 9781763606517
Subjects: Spirituality | New Age | Divination
Cover photo: Katla Ice Cave, Iceland - photographer, Andrew Poulos
Book Production Services: www.smartwomenpublish.com
Registered with the National Library Australia

All rights reserved. No part of this publication may be reproduced or transmitted in any form or by any means, electronic or mechanical, including photocopying, recording, scanning or information storage and retrieval system without the prior written consent of the publisher.

Disclaimer:

The material in this publication is of the nature of general comment only and does not represent professional advice. All material is provided for educational purposes only. We recommend to always seek the advice of a qualified professional before making any decision regarding personal and business needs. To the maximum extent permitted by law, the author and publisher disclaim all responsibility and liability to any person arising directly or indirectly from any person taking or not taking action based on the information in this publication.

We all have our own magic and power.

It is deep within us, and rarer and more beautiful than we could ever imagine.

CONTENTS

Preface 7
Introduction 13

1 Psychic Tools For Divination 15
2 Astral Travel 39
3 Tarot Cards 45
4 Automatic Writing 51
5 Predictions 55
6 The Merkabah Symbol 59
7 Timelines 65
8 Numerology Using Day Numbers 69
9 The Spiritualist Church 79
10 Connecting To Spirits 93
11 Working With The General Public 97
12 Animal Spirits .99
13 Psychometry .103
14 Crystals For Awareness 113
15 Crystal Grids .119
16 Crystal Singing Bowls 125
17 Light And Dark Energies 129
18 Mediumship .137
19 Spiritual Helpers 143
20 Gifts To Work With In Your Mediumship . . .151
21 Different Types Of Mediumship 157
22 Conducting A Seance 165
23 Spirit Rescue .179

24	Murder Cases And Missing Persons	185
25	Healing Cures For Mediumship	189
26	Spirit Signs	197
27	Vision Walk	203
28	Travel Is Good For The Senses	207
29	Past Lives	213
30	Precognitive Dreams	215
31	Toxic Spells, Manipulation And Energy Vampires	217
32	Spiritual Teachers	231
33	Superstitions, Curses And Negative Energy	235
34	Raising Your Vibration	249
35	Healing With Nature	257

Conclusion	267
Recommended Reading	269
About The Author	271
Contact Kerrie	273

PREFACE

Growing up in a small community by the sea on the south-east coast of Australia was, without doubt, a wonderful blessing. The coastal area where my family lived was surrounded by sprawling mountains that looked majestic on crystal-clear, brilliant days. From our front porch we had a view of the massive coastline, which was full of natural treasures: endless coves to discover and play in; beautiful, pristine beaches; and waves that were perfect for surfing, depending on the wind. On hot summer days we would all sit on the front porch, waiting eagerly for the southerly wind to come from across the sea and cool down the house, giving us some respite from the relentless summer heat.

My home looked normal enough, much like all the other houses in the ordinary suburb, but even on the hottest days, an unexplainable ice-cold chill would suddenly fill the house; it would silently work its way up my legs, like an invisible vine, then find its way to my bones. Then, just as mysteriously, it would disappear.

Night time was the worst and I dreaded going to bed. My home seemed to hold an extraordinary power; I felt the influence of an unknown, unrelenting, invisible supernatural being. I was terrified at night, and that fear has never left me; I'm scared of the dark to this day.

Eventually I learned that the house was haunted. There was a resident ghost, or lost soul, living in the manhole in our laundry. I had no understanding of spirits or ghosts as a child, but I quickly learned how to survive, as most children do. My defence was simple: I ignored the power, or ghost, or lost soul, or whatever it was. I simply shut it out and hoped it would go away. But this tactic only worked so far.

Every night, like clockwork, when the lights were out and everyone had gone to bed, I would hear the sound of heavy footsteps dragging their way from the laundry to my bedroom, where I lay shuddering with fear and dread. When the sound abruptly ended, I knew there would be a shadow standing silently beside my bed. A sudden coldness in the room would send chill waves all over my body and I found it hard not to scream. Feeling sick to my stomach and trying not to vomit, I would lie under the covers with my hand over my mouth, holding my breath. Terrified and shaking with fear, I would pretend to be asleep, hoping the 'monster' would go away.

To my dismay, this didn't work. The entity gradually became bolder, trying harder to get my attention by pressing down on me, almost to the point where I couldn't breathe.

One night when I was fast asleep, to my horror I was dragged by the elbow out of bed and onto the floor. In shock, I became completely paralysed; I couldn't move my body or cry out. After a while, crying and still shaking, I was able to crawl back into bed.

To my great relief, it all came to an end one night. Feeling brave, when the shadow appeared by my bed I peeked out from under the covers and stuck out my hand. I felt coldness, and saw hundreds of tiny black and grey dots in the form of a tall man dressed in a suit. Shocked, I jumped out of bed and, with strength I didn't know I had, ran to my parents' bedroom screaming, waking up the whole family.

Finally, my parents, with very little sleep and not knowing what to do with my so-called nightmares, insisted I stay in my own bed, but the deal was I could keep the bathroom light on. Everything seemed to change after that. It was like a miracle had occurred. I quickly learned that lost spirits thrive in the dark, so a simple thing like leaving the bathroom light on actually worked.

The offending nightly visits from the horrible spirit man in the suit, and other spirit traffic, finally stopped, although I could still sense silent eyes watching me all the time. My good fortune didn't last for too long, though, as my parents decided we had to visit my grandmother most weekends after that. The trouble was, the energy in the house became worse. It was cold, dark and totally lifeless, as if everything good had been sucked out of it. It was also full of wandering spirits that seemed to be everywhere; they even walked through the walls of the adjoining homes, going about their business without a care in the world.

I have also been able to clearly see visiting spirit people, or family members who had died. They would appear out of nowhere when we gathered at the round table in the kitchen for family dinners. On many occasions, spirit visitors popped in with messages of love.

One day I nearly fell off my chair when I saw a plump spirit woman wearing an old-fashioned dress appear behind my mother, warning her about her diet and telling her she was putting on too much weight. The spirit woman was my mother's mother, who had died of a heart attack when my mother was a child. When I relayed the message, my mother was not impressed, although soon after this she put herself on a strict diet and started watching everything she ate.

I had many experiences of seeing spirit people as plain as day, for instance, neighbours walking down the street even though they had been dead for years. One of these spirits was a sweet old lady, a widow who had lived at the bottom of the street with her two little dogs. A lovely, kind woman, she had let me play with her pets, which she said were her children. I will always remember watching her brush their teeth lovingly whenever they ate anything, saying she had never liked bad breath.

I also experienced different types of spirit phenomena, such as weird and pungent smells that came out of nowhere and lingered for days, like strong cigarette smoke, sickly aftershaves and strong perfumes.

The thing my mother hated most was my psychic sense, my 'knowing' things before they happened. Whenever I tried to talk to her about the things I saw, she would immediately shut me down and tell me it wasn't 'right'. She said it was rubbish, and it scared her.

As a psychic child, I never had anyone to help me, but loving spirit works in miraculous ways and will take great steps to look after its own. My saving grace came in the form of my invisible friend, or spirit guide, who called himself John. This kind, friendly gentleman spirit, who was only around in my younger years, was very protective. He was invisible, like most spirits, and I was the only one who could see and hear him.

I have spoken to many healers, psychics and mediums, and they have often told me they've had similar experiences. John had a very strong English accent, which I found hard to understand.

Years later, during my spiritual training, I learned he was the spirit of my grandfather, who had died in my grandmother's house before I was born.

My life as a spiritual medium so far has been a journey, with many lessons and much learning. As a sensitive child, I attended the local church every Sunday. It was like a celebration; it was a wonderful place to go once a week and catch up with other children. We were like a small family. We socialised happily and got on well together as we learned about the miracles and stories of Jesus from the Bible excerpts the teacher read to us each week.

The highlight of the day was when we all sang at the top of our lungs in the small choir, which made us feel extremely elated. This was my first experience with the energy and powerful healing effect of angels and the ascended masters, which I'm sure I began to channel back in those early days. The whole experience filled an empty space in me and resonated gently with my soul. The healing brought tears to my eyes, as I always felt so peaceful and happy within myself for days afterwards.

However, fate had me destined for other things. All of this came to an abrupt end the day a visiting evangelist took the place of our normal minister. Feeling safe, I made the mistake of telling her I could talk to dead people, and that I knew when things were going to happen. I also told her about my invisible special friend, John, who I liked to talk to when nobody was around.

Shocked, and with a nasty, frightening look of anger, the woman took a step back and screamed loudly in my face. She said I was an evil witch possessed by the devil. Instead of embracing me in her arms lovingly, she told me to pack up my things and leave that moment. I was no longer welcome in the church.

Horrified, I realised that my safe haven and new family were just an illusion. It was all crumbling down around me. I began to cry uncontrollably, as if I had done something terribly wrong. I felt like I was a really bad person. I was fourteen years old.

Metaphysical books were the flavour of the day back then, so I spent a lot of time in the local library, earnestly reading everything I could find to do with spiritual development, different esoteric philosophies, the paranormal, and the exercises that went with them. I was open to everything, to all types of paranormal experiences. But I still had a long way to go.

As a teenager, moving into the beach culture brought a whole new lifestyle, representing freedom and joy on so many levels. Nobody judged anybody else, and everyone did their own thing. My new friends were free-thinking, open-minded, very cool hipsters who were into New Age thought and meditation. They were a lot of fun and, best of all, loved nature like me. There were a few negative types, but I quickly learnt to navigate around them. It certainly was a welcome change from the former, very sheltered existence I had lived before.

I learned that nature in its purest forms, like surfing and swimming in the sea, grounds you to the earth, clears clutter from your busy mind, and slowly helps you feel energetically alive, connecting you to everything good in the world, no matter what you may be going through or how broken you may feel at times. It's a natural high, a great gift from spirit, and very healing. It can clear energy fields, which can sometimes get overloaded. It can take you back to a state of grace whenever you have any type of imbalance, like fear, chaos, stress, depression, or anxiety. Nature aligns you with your innate creativity on a soul level, opening doorways to all your senses.

INTRODUCTION

A *Medium's Story* consists of true information and case studies that come from my life as a medium in the community, working as a lightworker with the paranormal. I've combined some of my life experiences with step-by-step, easy-to-understand instructions on how to connect intuition with divination. The book is filled with successful techniques I have created and used over the years, and is peppered with real-life stories of hauntings, clearings, mediumship and the paranormal.

I believe we are all born with natural psychic gifts; it's just a matter of knowing how to use them. When you understand how your own natural gifts can help you develop your spiritual and psychic awareness, you can begin to use them as practical tools in your daily life.

You have a support team of angels and spiritual guides to help you along the way, offering protection and subtle guidance on your journey. When you consciously work on establishing relationships with your angelic helpers, you open yourself up to new opportunities you may never have imagined possible. With their love and ongoing assistance, you can find inner strength, overcome life's difficulties, and tap into hidden creative talents that have lain dormant and deep within your soul.

In the pages of this book, you will discover that you can predict the future, work with energies, and learn who your beloved spiritual guides are. The many practical and easy exercises, which are well tried and tested, will gently guide you through the process with divination and insights. As a result, you will help not only yourself but also your loved ones, your friends, and the larger community.

With love, patience, dedication and time, your awareness and psychic abilities will improve. Don't be surprised to find how easy it is; be encouraged by that, and you'll find that diligence and dedication will eventually take you to a more advanced level.

You will come to understand your life's purpose. You will learn to work with your master guides and angelic helpers. You will explore and understand the different types of mediumships and the gifts within yourself that you can awaken, and become aware of the different energies surrounding you—the light and the dark—and how to clear them. And last but by no means least, you will discover and learn to appreciate the importance and healing benefits of nature.

Within the pages of *A Medium's Story*, you will feel comforted to know that you are never alone. Your loved ones are always with you in spirit, and you have an abundance of angelic and spiritual energies to help you and guide you until it's your time to return once again to the spirit world.

1

PSYCHIC TOOLS FOR DIVINATION

In the early days of my psychic development, I learned to use many tools for divination, the practice of foreseeing future events or discovering hidden knowledge. These tools included many forms of scrying—using a medium to receive messages or visions—such as:

- Cloud gazing
- Crystal ball
- Black mirror
- Coffee cups
- Colours in the aura

I also learned the importance of meditation and timelines. At the same time, I was reading tarot cards, which give valuable insights and are generally very accurate. Somebody had given me a pack of tarot cards, and as soon as I picked them up I had a feeling of déjà vu, the sense that I had worked with them before as they felt so familiar.

However, it's a great responsibility to read for others. When you tell people the truth they often don't want to know, as they will always have their own agenda. I soon learned to be careful with what I said, as I quickly noticed that my friends took every word as gospel. As soon as my predictions came true, they would let me know right away. I always became extremely excited and felt like I was truly helping them.

To this day, my readings are always insightful, truthful and positive. I never tell people what they want to hear, just the truth, which some find quite disappointing.

My friends thought it was amazing the way I was able to download information so easily and talk about it in so much detail, even information about personal things they thought I couldn't possibly know. I always put it down to the fact that all people, events and actions leave an easily detectable energy trail, and this is equally true of past as well as future events. As soon as I looked at the pictures on the tarot cards, I had an inner knowing of what they meant. My newfound gift made me very popular, and before long I was in great demand.

I now put all this down to past lives. In a session with a past-life therapist, I learned that I had lived a lifetime as a woman called Margaret, who was a white witch and worked with tarot cards, herbs and other types of important healing tools.

As we carry memories in our subconscious minds from lifetime to lifetime, the information can be accessed quite easily from the soul's memory. It's the same for other things as well, like being able to pick up and play an instrument without ever having learned it, or speaking in another language without much study.

By developing your psychic abilities, you're placing your soul's energy, or aura, in contact with another's when doing any type of reading, and establishing a link or connection. I still find how it all works quite extraordinary.

With dedication to your craft, diligent practice, and a good teacher, you will learn how to still your mind, centre yourself, and tune into the other person's energy. After a while, the information will flow freely, and before too long you'll be able to freely access information from the other person's akashic records, which are universal events, thoughts, words and emotions in the past, present and future. Generally, your spiritual guide, which usually stands on either your left or right side, will assist in the process as well.

For those who are mediums, a loved one will always come through and give not only survival evidence, but also messages of love from the spirit world. We have many spiritual helpers in the spirit world to guide us every single day, and the good thing to know is that none of us is ever alone, even though it may feel like it at times.

In earlier times, medicine women, witches, wizards and the elders of tribes devoted their lives to ensuring the wellbeing and health of their communities. It was not uncommon for the wise ones of the community to work with burnt embers for divination; they simply stared into fires for visions, premonitions and future outcomes. This information was always passed on by the people of the time, who sought its gift for guidance and healing in their lives. While all of nature's elements were used in their practices, fire played an especially central role.

Even these days we can have many experiences in nature once we enter into that healing energy and realm. How many times have you seen strange faces on tree trunks when walking through a forest? Or faces and pictures looking back at you from the clouds in the sky? These are all messages from loving spirit, which is all around you, guiding you always, and letting you know you are never alone, not even for one minute.

Once you are open to the gifts from spirit that you are born with, you will find that scrying is a powerful tool that will open you up and develop the psychic abilities and innate gifts you have within you. There are also the ancient arts of crystal-ball gazing, black mirrors, coffee-cup and tea readings. It's also possible to read flour and rice: the person scatters the rice on a table and looks at the messages that are generally little pictures of things like flowers, animals, names or numbers.

Reading the lines of other things like stones, Chinese sticks, rocks and asparagus is also used by different cultures for opening the third eye, or psychic centre, in the body.

Cloud Gazing

Cloud gazing is one of the easiest ways of scrying for past, present and future events, and it's free. Besides exercising your third eye and opening up your imagination, it's a lot of fun. As a child, a favourite game of mine was watching clouds, and the pictures I saw fascinated me. When I first began to cloud gaze, I used to see angels, initials, faces and animals all the time. It's incredible what you can see, and how that can give you subtle messages for your own life. As for seeing angels, it's a beautiful thing, because once you open up to their world it will feel safe, and a reminder that you are not alone. Once you are aware of and open to things around you, the more you will see.

As a teenager, I used to lie on the beach with my small radio for hours, in the shade or under an umbrella, listening to music and gazing up at the clouds.

Another option was to go with my friends on long walks into the surrounding bush and sand dunes, find a shady tree, look up at the clouds and have fun by sharing with each other whatever information we got. I often saw things like numbers and initials, and it was fascinating to discover how often we all saw different things. There were so many faces, images and messages in the sky.

Cloud gazing was my fun, easy introduction to scrying. I have always believed it's just another way of spirit giving messages, which is similar to readings of coffee cups, crystal balls, and flat and dark mirrors. Spirit always gives us information, love and assistance in troubled times, as well as subtle warnings for us mere mortals on Earth having a human experience.

Clouds are a wonder of nature. There are up to ten cloud types, each type unique in shape and particular location in the sky. My favourite one would have to be the pink, orange and red clouds that occur at sunrise and sunset, and which are the result of the scattering of sunlight by the atmosphere.

LEARNING TO CLOUD GAZE

1. Make yourself comfortable on a protective towel or blanket. Lie on your back, making sure there's enough shade to cover your face, and don't wear sunglasses. Make sure you have a clear view of the sky and there is no obstruction.

2. Once you've done this, repeat three times, 'I ask spirit to open my mind and my third eye, and to show me pictures that I need to see to help me on my path.'

3. As you slowly start to see things, write them down. You may see faces, numbers, animals, buildings or other simple things.

4. When you start to do this on a regular basis you will see more. The more you use your imagination and have fun with the exercise, the more you will see. This will help your progression with your psychic abilities.

Crystal Ball

From as far back as I can remember, I have always been drawn to and loved crystals, including crystal balls, and for years I played the crystal bowls with clients for the healing experience. This art or process of seeing is one form of scrying, or crystal gazing, whereby images seen in crystals are interpreted as meaningful information. This information is then used to help people make important decisions in their lives about health, love and romance, finances, families, travel and much more. Crystals are also used in mentalism, which involves acts by stage magicians.

Crystal balls are made of clear or rutilated quartz, and to this day are common fortune-telling objects. They were used as far back as the fifth century in the Roman Empire, but were condemned by the early medieval Christian church as heretical. Crystal gazing was a popular pastime in the Victorian era, and was claimed to work best when the sun was at its northernmost declination. Immediately before the appearance of a vision, the ball was said to mist up from within, but I have never seen that. They are probably best known for their use by Romany people, who have traditionally used crystal balls to predict the future for their customers.

In other words, crystal balls have been used for thousands of years for clairvoyance and scrying. They certainly are great tools to use with psychic abilities, as they open the third-eye energy centre, or brow chakra, which is situated in the middle of the forehead and extends to the bottom of the nose.

My life as a medium and crystal-ball reader began when I was working full-time in shops, doing mediumship and tarot. I was always able to learn to read energy very easily, and with a crystal ball I was able to enhance and stimulate my natural abilities.

Many people believe the common misconception that crystal balls have magical powers. This is not the case, as the crystal ball is just a conduit of energy. It's used as a simple tool or doorway that enables the user to see images from their own subconscious mind.

Most people honour their crystal ball, don't like others to touch it, and often cover it with a dark cloth when not in use. It's also a good idea to put it in a safe place if used for divination. This way the crystal will be attuned to your energy only, and not that of curious others. It's also wise to give the crystal ball extra energy by placing it under a full moon, just to give it extra love, mystery and light.

Natalie

I received an email from Natalie, who said she wanted to give me the crystal ball her father had used as she had no use for it. I offered to pay for it but she insisted that all she wanted was to meet me. When I arrived to pick up the ball, I realised it was spirit intervention; I could see that Natalie was in desperate need of a reading. The poor woman said she needed an eye operation and was terrified she would end up blind like her mother, who was also in the spirit world.

Before I had a chance to gaze into the ball, Natalie's father came through, with her mother. The message was clear. Natalie was to stop worrying about everything. The operation would go well, it would be her last, and she would not go completely blind like she feared. Natalie told me it was the validation she so desperately needed. Natalie could not stop crying, and I could only imagine the fear and trepidation she must have been going through.

After speaking to Natalie's family in spirit, I cleared the ball with light energy and asked her to hold it for a couple of minutes so I could get a reading from her psychic imprint. Then I held the ball with a cloth and began to give her messages. The first thing I saw was a fox next to what looked like a building. When I told her this, she said she was thinking of selling her home as the upkeep was too difficult.

The fox, I said, was a warning that the people she was dealing with now were dishonest. If she did want to go ahead with the project, which she was still not sure about as she had lived there a long time, she would get better help with the sale of her property later on. She agreed with this and said she had been thinking the same thing.

At the end of the meeting, she hugged me so very tightly and thanked me for the advice and messages. She said she would definitely get some spiritual healing, like reiki, for her eyes and general wellbeing, as I had suggested.

Another time, when I did a reading for a woman, I saw a big cross in the centre of the crystal ball. This meant to me that her health would be okay, so I told her that whatever she was worried about was a waste of time. Not believing her ears, she jumped out of the chair and hugged me, crying, saying the message meant a lot to her as she was worried about cancer.

The crystal ball is a tool to provide service for psychic events, past, present and future. It assists in drawing out the psychic energy and focus to provide a reading. If you are psychic, yes, you can easily be taught, but not everybody has these gifts. Some may need to work harder than others to get good results.

Quartz, or smoky quartz, is in my opinion easier to read than clear glass, which can be more difficult for beginners. Quartz allows you to look into the layers of the natural inclusions.

Crystal-ball reading is not a religious practice. I am sure that in the Dark Ages it was, like most things, to do with the occult, but nowadays this work gives people insight, and empowers them to make the right choices for themselves. This is true of all spirituality.

It is also not a tool for diagnosis. As mediums, we are only reporting what we see in the crystal, and if that resonates with what our clients are seeing it is up to them to seek medical advice.

If you begin to see things you don't like, such as accidents or death, perhaps this practice is not for you, and it is your duty not to relay this unnecessary fear. You can attune the crystal ball by telling it you're not interested in seeing dark things or receiving negative predictions when you use it, as it does not have your permission. As lightworkers, we can advise people to be careful in their dealings, but telling them about horrible things will only evoke fear, anxiety and unnecessary worry. The client must be advised that their choices in life will often determine their own personal outcomes, and the insight you are providing them with in the reading will help them do this. I always say that if someone tells you something that doesn't feel right, always trust your own guidance, no matter who they claim to be.

READING A CRYSTAL BALL

1. Once you have selected the type of crystal ball you would like to work with, keep it in a safe space and make sure others don't touch it. I always like to keep a dark cloth over mine to keep it clean and protected from outside forces and other people's energies. I also have my own crystal ball I prefer to use just for myself.

2. Find a quiet space to work in so you won't be disturbed by outside energies and loud noises. I always call in the white light, and ask for a blessing and healing for the reading. To do this, I wipe white light around the ball three times. This cleanses it and charges the elements in the crystal, making it easier to read.

3. Allow the person you are reading for to hold the ball for a couple of minutes so it absorbs their energy and psychic imprint.

4. Holding the ball in your left or right hand, using a cloth so your skin is not touching it and you're not putting your own energy into the reading, rotate it slowly. You'll begin to feel your third eye opening up, and you may see small pictures and numbers in the ball. These visons will get stronger and stronger the more you concentrate, and you may even hear names in your head, or feel things for the client.

5. The more you practise reading the ball, the better you will be, as practice makes perfect. At first you may only see a few pictures, but over time, and the more you read, the story and information will get clearer, better and longer.

6. Remember to give positive information only. Never encourage any type of negative energy or information in your readings. Predicting death or sickness is against the universal laws and will only cause unnecessary stress.

    I have come across this type of reader before and often find they are only projecting their own misery. These days all my work, including tarot, mediumship and psychic readings, is by remote viewing because I gain the psychic link through the voice. This means I use the crystal ball remotely as well, and the client doesn't have to hold the ball or be in the room.

7. To gain psychic access to the person's higher self for the reading, with their permission simply say their name and ask spirit to help. Straightaway the ball will activate. You will see pictures, and receive clear and precise messages of the past, present and future clairvoyantly, as if the client was sitting in front of you in the room.

8. When you feel that the reading has come to an end, inform the person and place your ball in the cloth, then close down your energy.

Always remember to smoke, clear and cleanse your ball once a week. If someone gives you one as a gift, make sure you cleanse it to get rid of any residual energy that does not belong to you, as all crystals are strong energy amplifiers and carry energy.

I always cleanse my ball after each reading with clear white light that I visualise through my hand chakras in the middle of my palms. I rub my hands together to activate them. Alternatively, I place the ball under a full moon once a month, with excellent results. Some people like to charge their crystal ball with other crystals under a full moon as well, which is a beautiful ritual.

Black Mirror

The black mirror is another ancient tool used in the art of scrying. It is very effective, and is used mainly for invocation rituals and getting in contact with the spirit world. Some people believe it is evil but, again, this is a total misconception. It is easy and effective to work with, and it's amazing how much psychic information comes through such an ordinary tool.

Black mirrors were also used by witches to cast their spells for spell craft, the magical practices involving the casting of incantations. In older times, people used a bowl of water. The mirror is used for past, present and future events, and to communicate with spirits around you. It takes a bit of practice, but it is an effective way to really open up your third eye, like all types of scrying.

Mirrors can be round, square or oval in shape. For better results, you may like to use a vintage mirror, which has the capacity to go deeper. They say that the older the mirror the better the reading. In my practices, I often use a small magnifying makeup mirror.

Before working with my mirror, I like to cleanse it of residual energy by rubbing my hands together to activate the hand chakras, which are in the middle of the palms, then sweep it with white light that I visualise in my mind. When doing any work with spirit or divination tools, I always like to protect myself energetically with a bubble of white light wrapped around me. The white light is unconditional love.

USING A BLACK MIRROR

1. It's beneficial to work in a quiet place, and to have no reflections or bright light on the mirror. Some people like to work by candlelight.

2. Sit opposite your client and still your mind. Prop your mirror in front of you and tilt it so you can see the client's reflection, which will be upside down. This is the way you read their energy and aura; you only need to see their head and shoulders.

3. Ask your client to relax by taking three deep breaths in and out, and to begin to focus on being open to seeing what is around them. Ask them to stare into the mirror in a gentle, relaxed way.

4. As they do this, encourage them to look deeper into the depths of the mirror, almost as if they are looking through it. If there is any darkness, it will eventually disappear, or sometimes take on a grey or misty look.

5. You may see colours, shapes, symbols or moving images, but it's important to just concentrate. Some people will get information straightaway.

6. Before too long, while watching the client's reflection in the mirror, you will feel your third eye open and begin to see, hear or feel messages all around them. You'll also be able to pick up energy in their body. Remember, with any type of

work involving divination tools, be mindful that it will take a while so be prepared to be patient.

7. When the images, words, pictures or messages from loved ones begin to form, relate what you see to the client.

8. When you have finished working, tell your client that you have finished the reading. Close down your energy centres by imagining them as little lights turning off. When you've finished with the mirror, cover it with a dark silk cloth to protect it.

9. If working alone, stare at your face and you will see your facial features change, which is transfiguration in mediumship. These faces could be past lives, or they could be the faces of spirits, people you may have known, or spiritual guides you're working with. When you become more confident, speak loudly and call out to encourage the spirit world to come through closer so you have a better sense of who they are.

Debby

The first time I used a black mirror with a client, I was surprised at how easy it was. As soon as I tuned into the mirror, I saw the spirit of Debby's mother with a cigarette in her mouth, standing on the right side of Debby's head. I described the spirit to Debby and spoke to the spirit telepathically. She told me she had died of lung cancer. She also said she was a heavy smoker, but could never give it up as she loved it so much, even though she smoked strong cigarettes.

Talking to her further, she mentioned Debby's recent operation, when she had nearly died. Debby's mother said it had not been Debby's time, and my client, starting to cry, confirmed this.

I then saw travel for Debby, and a change of job, and was told by the spirit mother that her daughter needed to take better care of her health. As she said this, I started to gently burp with the energy coming through, and I could feel some type of past trauma and tightness in the region where Debby had had her operation. When I told Debby this, she said she had had thirty stiches in that area, and was still getting over the stomach operation from a few months ago.

Spirit always uses all the information you know to help you with your readings. I have a good understanding of the anatomy and physiology of the body from my former nursing days, so I knew Debby would be okay. More importantly, I could also see a bright future for her.

Some people have an understanding of astrology and numerology, and spirit will use these tools as well. This is easy to do via social media, like all readings, healings and clearings.

Claire

Another good friend of mine, Claire, who is also a medium, told me that when she lies in the bath and looks up at the steamy mirror, she can sometimes see her ex-boyfriend staring back at her. The father of Claire's eldest son, he was killed in a bike accident many years ago. She describes it as if she is going back in time, because he looks exactly the same as he did when they were teenagers, with his red beard, diamond earring and piercing blue eyes. It has given her so much comfort, healing and validation over the years to know that everything is okay and he is safe and doing well in the spirit world.

I've tried this myself on several occasions. The first time I did it, I saw my beautiful old cat Sofia, who died of an illness, looking back at me. I felt so much emotion as we had had such a strong, loving connection, even though I love all my animals.

Other times I have seen pictures of Europe come up in the mirror when I've been planning trips. I have seen spirit people I once loved, especially my aunty, and I could not believe my eyes when I saw a horse that I rescued one day when I was a child. It was a time in my life when I was always rescuing animals and birds, to my father's annoyance, and bringing them all home.

I have also seen spirit people sitting in the back of my car, through a misted car window, only to disappear again. This has given me a laugh at times, as spirit people always know what's going on in our lives and often like to pop in to let us know they are still connected to us.

Coffee Cups

Coffee-cup reading has been a tradition for many years, and the practice has often been passed down by someone in the family, or a friend or teacher. I was taught by a Turkish friend, who also reads tarot cards. It can be very entertaining, social and a lot of fun, especially with groups of friends or family, as well as at parties.

With practice, it is easy. Some people prefer tea-cup reading instead, but both methods work equally well; it's just personal preference.

These readings are always full of so much psychic information. Like scrying, reading the coffee cups involves interpreting symbols, small and big, that are formed by the coffee granules in the bottom and on the sides of the cup. I also like to read the small saucer. All the shapes, numbers and letters on the sides of the cup represent the future, and what's on the bottom represents the heart of the matter, or the current situation.

Turn the cup upside down. If the grounds at the bottom of the cup are very thick and murky, it may mean unnecessary worry, ill health or bad fortune, but this also depends on what the other symbols have to say.

For example, I did a reading for one of my husband's lawyer friends who was very successful in his career. Unfortunately, success can be a two-edged sword; his partners were jealous of his practice and wanted a piece of the action. It was never going to happen because they were not as talented as him, but this did not stop them from behaving in an underhanded way. When I explained what was going on, he laughed nervously and said it was true.

The bottom of the cup was thick and murky, which, in psychic terms, indicated turmoil. When I suggested to my husband's friend that he was probably drinking a lot, which was understandable with the stress he was under, he smiled cheekily and agreed. Luckily for him, I also saw three lucky clovers next to each other and could let him know he was safe and had nothing to worry about.

I advised him to not only stop drinking, but also to use protection, as I saw his work colleagues were attacking him energetically and going behind his back because of their jealousy.

At the end of the session, I had his spirit father and mother come in so they could hear what I was saying. They said they knew he was coming to visit us that day so had made a point of stepping in. With tears in his eyes, the man listened and thanked me for the reading, and for confirmation that his parents were good.

READING THE COFFEE CUPS

1. Prepare the coffee in a small pot. I prefer to use Turkish coffee powder, but you can also use Greek, which is just as good. Each one is easy to buy at most supermarkets, not expensive, and comes in a jar. To prepare, mix about three dessertspoons (how much depends on whether you like it strong) into some water in a small pot, with half a teaspoon of nutmeg or cinnamon to taste. Place the pot on the stove and cook until the liquid rises and is just about to spill over, stirring as you go so all the granules disappear.

2. Prepare your little cups and saucers and pour. Make sure the saucers and cups are plain and not patterned, as patterns can make it difficult to do the reading. Add sugar and milk if needed, as the coffee can be bitter.

3. After the coffee has been drunk, ask the client to turn it over onto the saucer and spin it slowly three times.

4. Wait about five minutes, then pick up the cup and place it next to the saucer, facing upward.

5. Pick up the cup with a cloth (optional), and begin to look at the symbols. From the handle, you will be reading from right to left around the cup.

    Generally, the bottom part of the cup represents people, situations, or ideas from the past, while the middle part on the sides of the cup represents the present. The top of the cup indicates what is approaching in the future. I like to look at the rim first and then divide the cup into sections of time around the cup: three months, six months, nine months and twelve months. For example, start from the right and look at all the symbols near the handle, which are the near future, and so on.

6. As you continue, you'll see different shapes. Triangles mean good luck. An angel with wings means protection. A dog may mean a loyal friend. A fox may not be a good omen; you might need to look at the other pictures inside the cup to determine this. A cat can mean deceit or quarrels. A snake can mean bad luck, or business problems, or that someone is going behind your back. Numbers can mean time. Initials are often names of people around you, or people coming into your life. A heart is a positive omen, like love in your life. A unicorn may mean magic around you and good fortune.

    If there is extra fluid that drips on the sides, it can mean tears, depending on what the feel of the cup is and what the other symbols are saying. Long and short lines often mean travel or a journey.

7. I also like to feel the cup the client has been holding; it will give me an impression of other things that may be going on in their life.

8. When you've finished reading the cup, have a look at the saucer and see what you get there.

9. When you've finished, close down all your energy centres. Wash your hands to avoid picking up any residual energy.

Remember, don't give bad readings, or gloom-and-doom predictions. This won't help anyone. As with all readings, to do this is negative and is against the universal laws. I'll never predict a serious illness, death or the end of a marriage. If there are problems, instead I suggest the client looks at the situation more closely.

Colours in the Aura

As part of my natural psychic development in my early years, I began to see rainbows around people's heads and bodies in beautiful, vibrant colours. I had no understanding of what they were. It used to make me gasp with wonder. It was incredible to see colours pop out of people's energy fields. I found that if I really concentrated, these fields would expand in density and last longer, instead of just appearing as a brief flash.

When I look at people closely, around their body they have what is called an aura. This appears white on first appearance, but if I look closer I can actually see colours. Each of these colours has meaning, and is connected to the chakra system or energy centres we have in our bodies.

Today it is possible to have your aura or energy field screened, offering valuable insight into the impact of the colours in your energy field, which can indicate chronic stress and warning signs of burnout. This enables you to take preventative action, both in your personal life and in your career, if necessary. Whether you use this screening tool out of curiosity, or as a diagnostic tool in alternative healing, it will always offer a valuable insight.

There are seven main major chakras, each in a specific location along the spine. These seven chakras are vortexes of energy that represent the seven levels of consciousness. The bigger and stronger the aura, the healthier the person. For instance, a clear, bright aura indicates a healthy, vibrant person, while a muddy or brown aura that appears thin, weak and shrunken can indicate emotional, spiritual and psychical health issues. This can create negativity, which can be caused by worry, stress, emotional turmoil, sickness or spirit entity attachment.

The first time I saw negative energy was at the top of a client's head in the crown chakra. When I mentioned this, he told me he was suffering from a type of depression; it was easy to see a large, brown heavy energy lingering on his head when he sat down.

Colours and their meaning:

- Red: Anger, selfishness, hate, a quick temper, power and energy. Alternatively, red can indicate vitality, ambition and raw sexual power. Over the years, I have seen flashes of this around the head, stomach and hip area.
- Orange: Sensuality and sexuality, pleasure, exercise, creativity, motivation, warmth, passion, balancing,

recovery from illness, pride. Sometimes I can relate this to past-life trauma as well.
- Yellow: Intellectual activity, power of the mind, higher intelligence of the body, study. I have seen a lot of this above the solar plexus area.
- Green: Balance, harmony, calmness, love, compassion, growth, healing abilities. I once saw a student with a green guide that was an angel. It stood on his right side and was working with him with his healing work. The student went on to be a very successful healer.
- Blue: Communication, expression, detachment, inspiration and information. This can also indicate new learning.
- Turquoise (New Age colour): Positive spiritual growth, new opportunities opening for spiritual learning. Amazingly beautiful colour.
- Indigo: Intuition, natural psychic ability and awareness, spiritual abilities. I have seen a lot of this over the years in students who are opening up to their latent psychic abilities.
- Lavender: Divine, master energy, softness, playfulness.
- Violet: Wisdom, pathway to enlightenment, the bridge between the mind and the higher mind, the bridge from the higher mind to the collective consciousness.
- Pink: Unconditional love, warmth, tenderness, modesty, gentleness, innocence, healing, empathy, selfless love, timidity, shyness.
- Gold: Higher self, brilliance, prosperity, spiritual radiance, higher creativity. In alignment with the energy of a master guide, such as an ascended master.
- Silver: Versatility, high energy, constant change, shape-shifter. I have seen this with 'star' people, who sometimes carry this energy or vibration.

- Brown: Indication that all is not well. Brown and murky energy indicates problems with clarity involving the emotional body.
- Black: Depression, wisps of sadness, evil, malice, sinister, low life-force energy, possible entity attachment. You usually know this colour is in the aura as soon as the person walks into the room because it comes with what I can only call a 'heaviness feeling'.
- Grey: Narrow minded, stuck in the past with emotions, conservative, depressed, low life-force energy, fear.

With practice, and an open mind and heart, the pathway of discovery is always opened for the student who works with unconditional love, and quality and energy of spirit. As you practise seeing these colours in the aura, you will discover a vast number of different shades of varied colours flash right in front of your eyes, as if by magic. This experience will open up your healing abilities, and the more you practise, the more you may find it helps you later on as a diagnostic tool with your healing work.

Always ask permission from the client, or the client's higher self, before commencing any work. I love using the colours of the aura as a diagnostic tool in healing, as they often show us energy or disease before it manifests in the psychical body, enabling us to seek help. Please note, however, that this type of work does not take the place of your own medical doctor's expertise.

SEEING COLOURS IN THE AURA

1. Have the client stand against a white wall that is not too brightly lit. Now, tilting your head back, begin to scan their auric field with your eyes, and notice qualities and characteristics such as size, shape and strength.

2. Ask the person to slowly count to ten, with a happy feeling, as this expands the aura. Look for the white energy around the outside of the body. It will look fuzzy at first, but with practice, and by lowering your eyes as if you are looking down, it will become easier to see it.

3. When you can see this, continue breathing slowly and feel yourself tuning into their energy.

4. You should now see sudden flashes of colour in front of you. Work around the head first, then continue going down, first to the shoulders and then to the lower body. Ask the person to think of a happy thought to increase their energy size as they breathe in and out.

5. To decrease the energy field, ask the person to think of a sad event; this will make the aura almost shrink or disappear.

6. While doing this exercise you will often see the outline of the person's spirit team, such as guides, angelic beings and sometimes relatives standing next to them. My own loving guide stands on my left side, but for others this may be different. The more you practise, the more you will see.

7. When you have finished, ask the person to close down their energy by imagining all their chakras, from the top of their body to their feet, closing down like little lights.

2

ASTRAL TRAVEL

The subject of astral travel has always interested me, since most of us travel when we go to sleep. When you travel, your spirit, which is connected to a golden cord attached securely to your body, departs from the body, roaming around the world and often meeting up with souls that you love and that love you.

I bought many books on the subject, and before long I was practising the exercise, locked in my bedroom. My first experience was not good. My mother kept calling me to come out of my room, disturbing me in the middle of my session. It was a horrible experience, to say the least, as I could feel myself leaving my body. As I listened to her screaming, my concentration was interrupted and I felt myself, for a second, stuck in the bedroom door. I quickly returned to my body, but I still remember the sensation and taste of the woodchips in my mouth.

Beth

A few years ago, Beth came to me and shared how one night she had had an amazing experience when she astral travelled back to her hometown in Canada. The family had moved to Australia and, feeling homesick, she used to cry all the time because she missed her best friend, and her old life and town. She felt like she had never fitted into Australian life.

One night Beth went to bed crying, heartbroken and sad, only to find herself suddenly having an incredible experience, which she described as an 'out-of-body experience', where she spontaneously astral travelled back to her hometown. Not believing her eyes, she looked around and saw herself in the town square where she had once lived. When she realised where she was, she travelled to her best friend's home. Overwhelmed with joy and emotion, she floated around, saw that nothing had changed, and immediately felt better.

This experience had helped Beth move on and let go of all the pain and sadness she was carrying. A few weeks later, her girlfriend wrote her a letter describing the strangest dream she had had, where the two of them had met one night in her bedroom and laughed for ages. Beth's friend couldn't get over how real the whole experience was and how wonderful it had been to connect with her good friend again.

Astral travel isn't anything new; it has been talked about since ancient times, throughout various cultures and religions. The idea comes from a 19th-century mystical system called theosophy, which claims that we have seven bodies, from the lowest physical body to the highest spiritual and mental bodies. Many people pursue an interest in astral travel as part of their spiritual development. As we explore, we learn that we are more than our physical earth suit, and astral projection reinforces this notion.

Astral projection is a term used in esotericism to describe an intentional out-of-body experience (OBE) that assumes the existence of a soul called an 'astral body', which is separate from the psychical body. This OBE is a wonderful tool for opening our awareness to the outer realms, as it connects us to a greater universal consciousness and aspects of our higher selves. It is extremely transformational, as it not only increases our awareness, but also our wisdom and inner knowing, or innate psychic abilities, which sometimes lie dormant within us.

Once you have activated this ability, you will be able to travel the cosmos, releasing any fear of death, which is just a transition to the spirit world and outer dimensions. It's very different from a near-death experience, as an OBE is an intentional experience.

An OBE is a transient state that some people have while conscious, when their self seems to become separated from their body, floats above the body, and looks down at the body from an elevated position.

Once you have learned to astral travel with an experienced teacher, you can harness the power of this phenomenon, and potentially travel anywhere your imagination desires.

The benefits of astral travel:

- Loss of fear
- Recognition of the self and immediate love for a higher perspective
- Increase of compassion, trust, faith and love of humanity
- Can be very healing as it increases the life-force energy and awakens subtle senses
- Helps us to be more creative as it raises our vibrational frequency

ASTRAL TRAVEL FOR BEGINNERS

1. Find a sacred space where you feel safe and secure, and choose a time when you won't be disturbed. Turn off phones and electrical appliances. Mornings are best, when you're not tired and have more energy. Never attempt to do this when you're tired or feel sleepy, or too early in the morning when you first wake up, so as not to go into the dream state.

2. When you have cleared your mind, lie down in a comfortable position with the firm intention that you can astral travel, and with the knowledge that you are safe. Clear your mind of any negativity and bad thoughts by affirming it is easy for you to do this and no harm will come from it.

3. Once you have done this, slowly visualise your astral body leaving you, but remaining connected to a silver cord inside you that acts like an anchor. Imagine there's a force right above you that's drawing your astral body away from your physical body. The secret is not to be afraid and just go with it. You may find that you are unable to move your limbs. This is called sleep paralysis. It's temporary, and is a sign that you are on par with the experiment.

4. Once you are out of your body, see your physical body beneath you. When you first begin, you'll find yourself in a state of nothingness and you will return to your physical body, but things will change after you repeat the process a few times. When you feel you've mastered this, try to focus on the desired location that you want to visit so you're not returned to your body without your consent.

Ideally, do a workshop with a good teacher, and talk to other people who have had different experiences. And remember that your confidence will grow the more you practise.

3

TAROT CARDS

Tarot cards are another tool for divination. When you learn how to work with them and understand all the different spreads, you'll be able to give readings for past, present and future events. I received my first tarot pack when I was a teenager and have never looked back. I've always been mysteriously drawn to the cards from the very first time I saw them, and I'm convinced I must have used them before, as they were so familiar. It didn't take me long to be able to read them for my friends, who, to this day, are always amused at the accuracy and in-depth information I give in all my readings.

The cards are a divine tool for divination and are perfect for insight, clarifying decisions, and obtaining psychic information. They would have to be a favourite of mine, as they are so accurate, and they enable me to learn and pick up psychic information all the time. By weaving all the beautiful images and pictures together from your pack, you'll become a storyteller, not only for yourself but also for your friends, family and clients.

Tarot cards have been around for centuries. I always have two packs, one for myself, which is sacred and only my own vibrations are on the cards, and one for friends and clients. The cards are not evil, as some people think, because you are only drawing on information from your own divine inner truth and knowing on a soul level. These people are coming from a place of fear, which, in reality, is simply misinformation.

You don't have to be a gypsy or a magician to read the cards. There are many different types of packs to select from these days, so I always advise my students to select one that's compatible with their own likes so they can easily relate to them. For example, I love the mythical tarot, as I love stories about ancient mythology.

In a tarot pack there are seventy-eight cards divided into two sections, major and minor. The twenty-two major arcana cards deal with the big events going on in your life and are part of your destiny, karma and spiritual contract for lessons and learning. The fifty-six minor arcana cards deal with how well you handle the lessons and day-to-day events.

Before working with the cards, a wise and practical move is to learn all the cards and their meanings first. Once you understand what the cards mean, your psychic abilities will kick in and you'll have more insight into what's going on in the other person's life. I also choose to not read reversal cards, and I keep my cards wrapped, or place a crystal on top of them when I'm not using them.

Tarot cards are an amazing tool to use with divination, and many excellent books on the market can assist you to learn the skills yourself. If you find that difficult, take a course. If you don't have the confidence or patience to learn alone, find a good teacher and sit in a group, as this will get you going. Remember, with practice you will get better and better.

When I first started, I learned all the cards and their meanings first, even though I already had a good understanding of them.

This gave me more freedom to channel information and allowed me more creativity. Since I wasn't looking at the meanings all the time, I was able to completely rely on my psychic abilities, tune into the situation, and just go with the natural flow of what I was picking up around the person.

Before I start readings, I do my usual ritual of placing protection around myself. I cleanse the cards with white light to release residual energy. I visualise white-light energy running around the cards and tap the packet three times, as if to activate them. Some readers blow on them three times, as if waking them up and getting them ready to work.

You can also smoke the cards if you've been busy with many clients. This will cleanse them and clear them of any residual energy, especially if they've been handled and shuffled by many people. I prefer to work with my own cards and don't like people touching them, but this is just my preference. I don't need the client to shuffle the cards as I can tune in and read the energy anyway. I learnt this by doing many remote phone readings and working on social media over the years.

USING THE TAROT CARDS

1. After shuffling the cards, separate the pack and work with the major arcana cards first, by pulling a card daily. Then start to increase your spread by using three cards, representing past, present and future, for any insight into a question or situation. It's amazing what you can receive.

2. As you play with the cards when doing readings for yourself, you will begin to gain more insight into the meanings by relating them to yourself and what's going on in your life.

3. Move on to the minor cards, which represent everyday events. When you're feeling confident and the cards have become familiar, work with the suits of the minor cards, then the people cards, until you have a good idea what they all mean. It's a waste of time just reading out of a book because you want to get the creative and psychic energy flowing.

4. When you've finished reading the cards, keep your favourite spreads wrapped up, or place a crystal on top of them. I use a big piece of rose quartz for its loving qualities, but it depends what you are drawn to.

5. Close down your energy by closing down your chakras.

Tarot cards can be another good way to psychically link to the spirit world. Once you've made the link with the spirit person, just go with it without using the cards any longer; this will take you to another level. For example, sometimes I'll be doing a spread when suddenly I can feel a spirit approaching. I will then hear them talking, as I'm also clairaudient.

Don't let anyone tell you that you have only one gift, as we often have many. If you're a psychic, healer or medium, of course you can work with and blend the different energies together. Your intention is to work at your highest potential for the client, who is asking for guidance.

In my earlier development, a teacher told me I had to make a choice about being either a medium or a psychic, but intuitively I knew that this was not the case. What the teacher was saying did not ring true to me. The first feeling that struck me that day was that the teacher was talking about his own limitations and beliefs. I found out later that he did not like people progressing, and would do anything to stop them from working and being successful.

It's my belief that you should follow your own intuition using the gift spirit gives you, which is always to work at your highest potential. I knew I was right to question this particular teacher. It was just another lesson in boundaries with some of these spiritual teachers that come into our lives for lessons and learning. People sometimes forget that we work for spirit.

Lexy

Lexy was a woman in her forties who had booked in to have a reading over the phone. As soon as I started speaking to her, I asked her if her mother had passed as I could hear a woman talking in my ear, telling me she was Lexy's mum, and that she had died of a sudden heart attack. Then, as I felt the spirit come closer, I described what I saw in my mind's eye: a big-breasted woman with a sunny disposition, straight hair that she wore in a ponytail, wearing a lovely floral dress that came down to her knees. The woman also said that she was a widow and was with Lexy's dad in spirit. He had passed of cancer a few years before her.

As I spoke to the spirit woman, I could feel a terrible breathlessness and pain in my heart as she went on to describe how she had died. She had several messages for Lexy, who was over the moon to hear from her mum.

When the spirit woman had finished talking, I pulled out the tarot cards and gave Lexy a tarot reading. Through the cards, I was able to see that she would soon start a new business, and her dreams of working with children would one day become a reality, but she had to first start believing in herself as she had always lacked confidence.

As I did the reading, I could still hear the spirit woman in my ear, thanking me and agreeing with what I was saying. That made me smile.

4

AUTOMATIC WRITING

Automatic writing is the process of obtaining information from the subconscious mind, or higher self, by spontaneous or involuntary writing. Your initial efforts may result in illegible and disorganised scribbling that's impossible to understand, but with practice it will improve. As you develop your psychic awareness, your skill at automatic writing will improve. It may take time, but with patience and practice you will get there.

When you first begin, you may just get words, but then you'll get phrases, and then sentences. You may even start with figures or symbols. Listen only to the loving and caring voice that you hear within your mind, as this represents the energy and entities that come from the divine source, or what we call the 'light'. Any thought or voice that sounds harsh, negative or angry, or comes with a not-right energy needs to be sent back into the light. This is not the energy you're looking for. Remember, be patient with yourself.

In my early development, I was able to draw a picture of my own spirit guide, White Feather, who spoke gently to me through my ear chakras. This was an incredible experience. Not only did I get to know and see what my guide looked like, but from that day forward I was also able to develop a loving and trusting friendship. There are many psychic artists in the world today who also love to draw images of loved ones and guides, and the accuracy of their drawings can be incredible.

Like everything when working with the spirit world, automatic writing requires time, patience, meditation and a safe, serene atmosphere in which to work. I always prepare and clear my space with white light, or sage or incense burning to create the type of space I need.

PRACTICE FOR AUTOMATIC WRITING

1. Sit in a comfortable position, in a place where you will not be disturbed (your own sacred space would be ideal) and light a candle. Make sure you're sitting up so as to keep your chakras in alignment, which will also help you stay awake. A good solid chair with a back is ideal.

2. Bring down your protection of white light and wrap it all around you.

3. Centre yourself by breathing in and out, relaxing your whole body and emptying your mind of any clutter or worries from the day, remembering that this is a special time for you. Soon you will be able to hear words, or have a feeling of words that you want to write down

4. At the top of your paper, you may want to ask a question that you need help with. Now close your eyes and meditate on the question in your mind's eye, holding your pen in your normal writing hand, or having your fingers ready on the computer keys.

5. When you begin to get the information, start writing it down. If it comes too quickly, ask your spirit guides to slow down. Imagine that someone else is controlling your pen or even guiding your hand.

6. When you feel the session is finished, thank your spirit guide and angel helpers for their assistance, then close down by gently imagining all your chakras, or energy centres, as little lights being switched off.

7. Now imagine yourself anchoring to Mother Nature, and bring yourself back into the room. You may not be successful the first few times, but like anything, this process takes practice. Over time your pen will flow freely and you'll be amazed at what you get. At first you may get names or numbers, or even a scrawl, but as you continue you will improve and begin to get words, and even messages and stories.

5

PREDICTIONS

In my career working for the media, I have made many predictions about world affairs, famous people and various outcomes, if it suits me and if it's for the person's higher good. If it will bring ridicule or harm, I won't do it. For instance, I won't give outcomes for horse racing, which is something I detest because it's my belief that the sport is cruel. Over the years, I have met many animal communicators and healers who have worked with racehorses, and they have spoken to me about the sometimes cruel and terrible treatment of these majestic animals. It's my firm belief that animals are companion souls and are here to teach us unconditional love. They have chakra systems as well, and emotions.

I will also never predict death, or give negative outcomes, as that is against the universal laws, but I will give subtle suggestions about health issues. Generally, the client will know themselves, but they could have their head in the sand.

A prediction is a statement about the future. Most people use tools, but the best way to predict is just to clear your mind and be open to seeing what comes through, making sure to write it down straightaway as this is spirit information.

I have made many predictions over the years and many of them have come true, including situations in the British royal family and ongoing problems in the Middle East.

A good way to begin predicting is by looking at photos of images, countries and people you know. You can also get surprising impressions and feelings by looking in magazines. It's like when you meet somebody for the first time—first impressions are always correct. When you still your mind, it's easy to read people or get impressions. Sometimes you can see them wearing a 'mask' and you know it's not the real them. Once you clear your mind and ask about something in particular, you will often see a little movie, or pictures, with feelings and answers and outcomes.

When this happens, it's best to write it down so you will remember it, as the messages will often come from your guide or a loved one in spirit. If you don't like what you see, detach, ask spirit not to give you any more information, and close down. Something to remember is that the timing with predictions can sometimes be delayed.

With patience, I learned to slow down my brain and focus on things I desired, and wanted to do in my life. I've always been an active person, and in the past, when I was much younger, I found it hard to concentrate and pronounce words because my brain has always been so fast. To be honest, it was hard at first, but over time, and with perseverance, I managed to get to my goal and received many rewards on the way. I gradually learned to focus and connect to the inner world of spirit and use my psychic gifts more effectively.

Not only will meditation help you focus so you can do more in your daily life, but it will also teach you to become calmer, more relaxed and more successful. It will also ground you so you can work at your highest potential, which will also benefit everyone around you and have a positive influence on others you come across.

Meditation also helps with negative mindset chatter, which, if not watched, can attract negative people who are similar to the destructive energy you may be engaging with. Once you learn this easy process, your life will become more rewarding as it helps you to go with the flow.

6

THE MERKABAH SYMBOL

Through my interest in the environment, nature, and now climate change, I was grateful to be introduced to the energy of the merkabah, an ancient symbol used in sacred geometry, which uses geometric shapes that have a deep metaphysical meaning. I often use the merkabah symbol, which means light or spirit body, with my healing work as it is so powerful.

The symbol is made up of two intersecting tetrahedrons that spin in opposite directions, creating a three-dimensional energy field that provides protection and light to the individual. Through my discussions with like-minded friends, we learnt to activate this symbol, or vehicle of light, through meditation, prayer and visualisation. It provides protection when doing any spiritual work and can take you to higher dimensions very safely.

The merkabah reminds us of the potential power we can utilise when we unite our energies in pursuit of healing and spiritual growth.

During 2019, I went through what I can only describe as one of the saddest environmental disasters of my lifetime, the bushfires in Australia. After witnessing the death and devastation of so much wildlife, losing people I knew who had died, and watching people lose everything they had worked hard for their whole lives, I felt that as an empath I had to do something to stop the pain, bring rain, and provide some relief for the horror that was happening at my back door. It was energetically killing me.

For many years, I had played with the merkabah symbol. I used it as a safe vessel, or type of ship, in meditation by riding it like a surfboard, or sitting in it snuggly and taking it high into the surrounding clouds so I could manifest rain in places that my country needed. To make this happen, I asked the four elements, or nature spirits, for help. Over time, it worked for me, whether by chance or just luck I'm not sure, but I am an open-minded person who likes to create new possibilities.

On my first attempt after the bushfires, I think it rained three days later and did its job. Unfortunately, it did not bring back the lives of the wild birds and animals that had died. I covered that with the healing energy I sent to the area to help wounded souls move on, with the help of the archangels.

I have to confess that, since the merkabah is so solid and safe, I've also used it for remote viewing, teleportation, and a type of time machine to take me into the future and the past.

RAIN MEDITATION USING THE MERKABAH SYMBOL

1. For the ritual, light a large white candle and scatter fresh flowers around you.

2. Sit in a comfortable position in your sacred space where you will not be disturbed.

3. Hold a clear white quartz in your left hand, with the intention of healing, and a rose quartz for love in your right hand to amplify the energy you're working with.

4. When you're ready to begin, take three deep breaths in and out, letting go of any negativity, dark thoughts, sadness or blockages from your mind, spirit and emotional and psychical body. As you do this, you will feel yourself relax.

5. Slowly visualise a golden light of love and pure energy radiating around you and caressing your whole body, making you feel safe, protected, loved and secure.

6. Slowly visualise roots or plants coming out of the bottom of your feet and slowly travelling down to the earth star, anchoring your energy deep into the earth to ground you. The more grounded you are the higher you can go.

7. As you breathe slowly in and out, you will feel your consciousness expanding. Breathing steadily, visualise your energy coming up to the colours of the chakras, first a beautiful red colour, then orange, then yellow, moving slowly up to green, then aqua blue, indigo and finally purple. The colour will finally reach the transpersonal point (gold) and you will feel all your energy points in alignment.

8. Imagine wrapping a beautiful white light around you for protection.

9. In your mind's eye, imagine sitting inside an open merkabah symbol. With your intention, command and feel the sacred image as a chariot with a super engine, wrapping its energy all around you, until you feel you are safely in the centre and fully protected within the walls.

10. Command your chariot to rise high into the sky until you reach a large white cloud that can be filled with rain for the thirsty earth below.

11. Now call on the four elements—earth, fire, wind and water—to fill the clouds with rain. Repeat three times: 'I now ask for mother earth's help in making rain'. As you do this, send loving energy to the earth.

12. Now call on the guardian angel Matariel, which blesses the earth with rain, to open up and stop the fires; help the thirsty, dry nature; soak the ground with rain; fill the rivers with water to relieve everything that has been suffering for too long.

13. Once you have done this, it's time for you to call in the archangel Raphael for healing the suffering in the world. These beautiful beings are here for assistance and will work in great harmony with the elementals. Like all sentient beings, they offer you not only assistance, but also love and encouragement. All you have to do is thank them for their assistance.

14. When you feel that you have finished sending energy, it's time to return. Ask the merkabah to return safely back to the ground. As it does, you will feel it open and call back all your energy. Don't forget to ground yourself.

15. You have just had an interesting experience, and now it's time to come back into your body and close down all your energy centres, or chakras. You can do this meditation as many times as you want, or only when it is warranted. Remember, you can travel anywhere in the world with this simple meditation.

7

TIMELINES

When I was a teenager, we used to play a game called Timeline to see how we would manage in the future and discover what the outcomes would be. With a bit of practice, it's a fun thing to do. You will find that there can be all types of outcomes, and it will give you a reality check to see if you're on the right path in life. You can do this by yourself or with a friend.

CREATING A TIMELINE FOR YOURSELF

1. Get yourself into a comfortable position in a sacred place you use regularly for meditation. Make sure you won't be disturbed, and you are comfortably dressed and feeling relaxed.

2. Take three deep breaths in and out until you feel yourself letting go of any stress, worry or anxiety you may have been feeling. As you do this, you will feel yourself relaxing completely. You have no fears, no worries; you're just letting everything from the day go. You are safe, you are secure and nothing bad will happen to you.

3. Now gently count down from ten to one, and with each breath you take in, you will feel very sleepy. When you get to one, you will be totally relaxed and in a meditative state.
   - Ten: You can feel all the stiffness in your body relaxing, starting with your feet. Let them relax. Feel yourself becoming more comfortable as you slowly breathe in and out, in and out.
   - Nine: Moving up from your feet, you will feel your legs relaxing; they will begin to feel heavier and heavier.
   - Eight: Feel the relaxation spreading up to your stomach, then making its way through your whole body. You have such a comfortable feeling as you let go of all the tightness and rigidity you've been storing in all your muscles.
   - Seven: Feel the relaxation spreading down your arms, neck and shoulders.
   - Six: Your eyes feel heavy and you want to go to sleep, but you're concentrating all your thoughts and attention on your breath as you drift deeper and deeper into relaxation.
   - Five: You are now totally relaxed. Even if you tried, you would not be able to move your body because you are so relaxed and sleepy, letting go of all the stresses of the day.
   - Four: Concentrate all your thoughts and attention on your body. Feel the gentle waves of relaxation running through your body, helping you drift deeper and deeper, deeper and deeper. You have no fears, no worries. You are safe and secure.
   - Three: As you breathe in and out, you feel totally relaxed, comfortable and secure.
   - Two: You are now totally relaxed. Nothing can disturb you.
   - One: Now imagine you are in a beautiful garden. You can feel the warm, soft sun shining down on your skin, you can see the blue sky above, and you are surrounded by an array of trees and a variety of coloured flowers.

As you stand in this beautiful garden, imagine, in your mind's eye, a straight blue line going off into the future.

4. As you position yourself on the line, in your mind's eye walk three months into the future. When you have arrived, feel and see what it looks like.

5. Go further and take yourself six months into the future, remembering everything in great detail.

6. It's time to move even further into the future. Take yourself forward one year. How do you feel? What do you see around you? Remember, you are in control and no harm will come to you.

7. Now take yourself two years into the future. How do you feel? Can you see other people who are important to you? The future is yours. What have you made of it? Remember that you are safe, you are secure, and you are in control of your destiny. You are now living the best life possible for a better future. Nothing is a problem as your life gets better and better because you feel loved.

8. In a moment you will count from one to three. On the count of three you will open your eyes and feel better than you've felt in a long time.
   One: You feel all the energy coming back into your body.
   Two: You are now feeling lighter and more awake.
   Three: You are wide awake.

If you guide another person in doing this exercise, let them slowly tell you what the experience was like when they come back into the room. Ask if they have any questions. Reassure them that they are always in charge of their destiny. Encourage them to always trust their intuition, as it is never wrong, and it will lead them to where they are meant to go for their higher selves.

8

NUMEROLOGY USING DAY NUMBERS

Numerology is the study of numbers and the energetic influence they have in a person's life. Numbers offer insight into their unique characteristics, future events, and life's purpose. It's amazing how much information you can get just by knowing and understanding a person's day number.

A day number is derived from an individual's birthdate, and represents specific personality traits and tendencies associated with that day. It reveals the qualities and characteristics that shape the person's behaviour, and the way they approach situations and life in general. Just by knowing someone's birthdate, you can get a good understanding of the way they operate in the world. It can also offer a psychic link, since it's a way of tuning energetically into the person's energy when they open up.

Simply add up the numbers and you can find out a lot. For example, somebody born on the tenth day of the month is a day-1 personality type (10 = 1 + 0 = 1). Someone born on the fourteenth day is a day-5 personality type (14 = 1 + 4 = 5).

The process is easy to learn, and it will help you understand the family, friends and clients you have in your life.

Personality types

Day-1 personality type
1, 10, 19, 28

This personality type is born to lead. These people are very independent, hardworking, prefer to work on their own, don't like to be told what to do, and like to run things their own way. They like to be in control and tend to call the shots in most situations in their lives. To be micromanaged would be difficult for them, as in most instances they are capable of doing whatever job is at hand. They have great ambition and a strong drive for success. Natural leaders, they are extremely self-dependent. They can also be egoistic, dominating and stubborn, and can become easily frustrated by the same routines, making it easy for them to move on. Once they make up their mind about what they want, they're able to move forward with great determination and success.

Affirmation

I always know that I am safe and secure since I trust my own judgement, wisdom and feelings. I don't rely on others to give me information or tell me what to do. I believe that great spirit supports me in everything I do. I am always open to sharing my life with new people and exciting opportunities. Life is to be explored.

Day-2 personality type
2, 11, 20, 29

These people are generally the peacemakers. They are peaceful and spiritual, and usually avoid arguing or even disagreeing with others. They are warm and affectionate, and can be very diplomatic, patient and tolerant unless they feel that they're under some type of threat. They are sensitive people and can be kind, but they can sometimes suffer from mood swings. This can lead to depression, which can be hard for them to manage at times. They also have keen powers of observation, good intuition, and, having a strong sense of empathy, can recognise the inner needs of people around them. When they trust the people in their lives, they are happy to share their inner world.

Affirmation

I trust the process and let go of all my fears. I am always happy for others, as I understand that these positive feelings will bring good karma and positive energy into my own life. I find joy in understanding the needs of others, and it brings me great satisfaction to work in service for spirit always, as I understand the teachings and spiritual rewards that will come back to me. I surround myself with beauty and live my life simply; I never go without. I am safe, protected and secure always.

Day-3 personality type
3, 12, 21, 30

The number three is supposedly a lucky, auspicious number. These people are what I call the 'builders' of the world. They are practical, good thinkers and tend to take their work seriously, leading to success, even though it might take them a while to get there. It's no surprise they are highly creative, and have a good sense of harmony and appreciation of art in everything they do. They also have an eye for beauty. Hard workers, these people are also social and fun loving, and love their freedom. They don't like to feel restricted in their personal relationships; they need their space and don't appreciate being controlled or confined. They often seek relationships where they can have their personal freedom, and they will offer the same to their chosen partner.

Affirmation

I appreciate my freedom and have great joy in discovering new things every day. I love to create things in the world. I love to be busy, and I enjoy my success and my creativity, which flow freely through my veins. My world is my oyster and I enjoy the rewards I attract so easily in my life. I see these as nothing but great blessings that I love to share with others in my life, including my family.

Day-4 personality type
4, 13, 22, 31

These people have a lot of energy. They are also very down to earth, but can sometimes get in the way of themselves because they can have difficulty making up their minds; they have a tendency to overthink things. Too often they will keep their brilliant ideas under wraps. They are also sharp minded, honest, trustworthy, loyal, powerful and well-organised, and take all their responsibilities very seriously. They are known to be good leaders, and have excellent organisation skills. Their personality makes them good speakers. For this type, relaxation and freedom from life's worries are the keys to a harmonious life.

Affirmation

The power of the great universe supports me every day, in everything I do, think and say. It's easy for me to do things, as I have an abundance of energy and I love to build solid foundations in my life. I have a healthy mind, body and spirit, and have copious amounts of love in my life. When I believe in something that I am deeply passionate about, it comes to me easily.

Day-5 personality type
5, 14, 23

These people are quick thinkers, kind, intelligent, confident, charismatic, energetic, adventurous, curious, restless and very creative. They often have fast minds. Most are independent and don't like to be told what to do; they love having a sense of freedom. They have excellent communication skills, and excel in whatever business or other endeavour they choose to have in their lives. They have the mindset that says: There's nothing I can't do. These types can also become bored easily, and can be restless or fickle, and this can lead to making bad choices. They may also allow the wrong people to ride on their coattails. They love nothing better than new and exciting experiences they can learn from.

Affirmation

I have the freedom to welcome change, and am not afraid to walk away from difficult friendships or toxic situations that no longer serve me for my highest good. I'm always supported by loving spirit, and walk my path with confidence always, using all my spiritual lessons and contracts to forgive those who have hurt me. I'm not afraid to try new things and I welcome change, always rejoicing in the new with great gratitude. I love to be creative, and to build my own successful world for anything I desire that makes my heart sing.

Day-6 personality type
6, 15, 24

The ruling planet of number six is Venus. Day-6 people are gentle, caring and considerably kind. Love is very important to them and their main focus is on relationships. They are beautiful souls, responsible, strong and compassionate. Their loving attributes mean that they like nothing better than to nurture others, including family and friends. They're attracted to the beautiful things in life. They are known as homebodies, and are very protective of their inner circle. They attract all the comforts in life with their magnetic personalities. Their spiritual role in life is to help others, and they do what they can to make the world a better place.

Affirmation

My home is my castle and my strong foundation in life, which is full of beauty, light, music and love. Everything around me is in total harmony and balance, and this is the reason I want for nothing, and everything is always in perfect harmony. I care deeply, and my life is abundant and easy. I am totally loved by everyone around me.

Day-7 personality type
7, 16, 25

These people are very spiritual and insightful, and meditation can help them in all aspects of life. Too often, though, they can make the wrong decisions when they don't listen to their intuition, learning things the hard way. One of their lessons in life is faith: how to be still and listen to their inner soul. They have a tendency to hang on to things, and need to learn to let go. On a positive note, they search for deeper meanings in life than what is obvious on the surface.

Affirmation

I always trust my gut and listen to my intuition when things don't go well for me. I always have faith in spirit and the universe as I know this is the best way to live my life, and to be in alignment with my higher self, which is my inner wisdom. I trust in my natural gifts always, and live my life with great passion and light. I am always safe and secure, and never go without.

Day-8 personality type
8, 17, 26

These people are good in business; they like to run their own show and know how to make money. They have sound judgement, are good communicators, and their lesson is to learn about balance and power. As ambitious souls, they love to be successful with anything they throw their energy into. They thrive on the positive energy they're able to manifest, and with their desire to go into any area of enterprise. They are self-confident, have an inner wisdom that can help not only themselves but others as well, and they have love for humanity. It can sometimes take them a while to align themselves with the right partner, as they don't always make their choice for the right reasons.

Affirmation

It's safe for me to trust my natural abilities with my choices in business. I understand it's important to be patient and not jump into relationships too quickly. I'm in control of my life and all my affairs. I'm able to blend in with the natural flow and energy of universal success, and I welcome this into my life as I believe it is my right to do so. I also think of others less fortunate, as the more I give out comes back to me tenfold. I am the creator and director of my own reality as I am powerful and prosperous.

Day-9 personality type
9, 18, 27

These people are imaginative, passionate and creative. They also have global awareness and are here to help humanity. They are practical people and often work behind the scenes, but they are still able to make a mark on society with their convictions and spiritual beliefs. The more they help the world, the more spirit helps them walk a good path with a good life, where everything is taken care of no matter what the odds. Their most important lesson is to release what no longer serves them, especially their temper, and move on to the next challenge, thus beginning the journey again. This includes relationships as well, because what they give out will come back to them karmically always.

Affirmation

I walk my spiritual path with great conviction, as I know it is my destiny. I am one with the universal flow of life, and trust in the highs and lows it brings to life's lessons. I am here in service to mankind. I play by my own rules. Once a cycle is finished, I'm able to learn from it and move on without any problem. I am safe, secure and always looked after. I look forward to my next adventure and spiritual cycle as I know I am exactly where I am meant to be.

9

THE SPIRITUALIST CHURCH

When I felt I was on my true path of discovery with my gifts, I wanted more, as the spiritual energy flowing through my body was driving me more and more into the spirit world. One day a friend told me to go to the spiritualist church, where I would be able to find information about the spirit world, including how it worked, and learn to work with my natural abilities as a medium, which were becoming stronger the more I tapped into them. My childhood memories of the horrible spirit man that lived in the laundry roof still plagued me and tormented my mind, so I needed to talk to somebody who understood such things.

By this stage, I had accepted that I was different from most people. I was reading lots of paranormal books and learning as much as I could. When I discovered the spiritualist church it was a blessing, to say the least. It was an initiation into another world and it helped me find my community. I discovered that there were people like me, from all walks of life, who also wanted to know more about the spirit world and what it had to offer.

The minister who helped me back in those early days was a medium and clairvoyant who ran the church. She was a kindly woman, well into her seventies, but she appeared ageless. I've often found people that truly work for spirit have a lot of energy and are very youthful. Smiling, the woman said I had a long way to go. But then she laughed and told me she could see my life was about to change in an amazing way. She taught me to believe in my abilities and myself, and she had a profound influence on me that I am grateful for to this day.

As you learn to work with your gifts and powers, you will gain confidence. Everything will become much easier over time. Your ability to tap into things will give you great insight into your inner world and the world around you. The more time you take to work on yourself, the more you will be able to release negative patterns and karma, by connecting and working with your higher self and increasing your own karmic cycle.

My first impression of the church was overwhelming. I was having weekly experiences of the paranormal that I could not explain, but I could feel myself opening up like a flower. Being introduced to the church was truly the beginning of my spiritual journey and my path as a spiritual medium.

Over the years I had become used to seeing spirits or dead people hanging around, but I had never seen so many packed to the rafters, all in one place. I also had no idea I could actually communicate with them. Everything began to make sense.

As I looked around the room in awe, I saw great gobs of spirit energy whirling and swishing around in the air above people's heads. As the congregation sang, they built up the energy to create a bridge, or link, to the spirit world, making it possible for the medium sitting at the front of the church to connect to loved ones on the other side, who were all waiting so patiently to bring messages of love to their loved ones in the congregation.

In my years of working in the spiritual church I learned many things, including protection, grounding, closing down, spiritual healing, meditation, overheads, crystals for protection, and so much more.

The Importance of Protection

One of the first things I learnt when first starting out as a young medium was protection and the importance of closing down my energy at the end of working with spirit. It's also important to use protection when doing any type of energy work and working with spirits. As sensitive souls, we all need this in the world as a second skin to stop any unwanted and toxic energy that may upset us.

White light is the universal energy—loving, gentle and positive—and when visualised and used it provides the highest degree of spiritual protection from negative energies. It is powerful and the best protection in the world, as it is unconditional love and can provide the greatest healing on so many levels. White light can be used by anyone and is particularly important for empathic people to use, as it shields you from the effects of feeling the emotions of others. It's very simple, and anyone can use it no matter their faith or religion as it's pure, unconditional universal love.

USING WHITE LIGHT FOR PROTECTION

1. Gently close your eyes and, taking three deep breaths in and out, ask spirit to surround you with white light. If you're using the white light for protection, envision it coming down over you and enveloping you so you're in what appears to be a protective bubble.

2. Once the white light is surrounding you, state your intention. For example, 'Protect me from the negative energy I will encounter today.' There are many different mantras and chants available for you to use.

3. As you sit with your eyes closed, still breathing slowly and deeply, visualise the white light as it travels to each chakra in your body. Allow it to cleanse each chakra until you feel light, and visualise it moving on to the next.

4. Surrounding yourself in white light like this will ensure that you aren't affected by people who are draining your energy. You know who they are.

The process for self-healing is just as simple, but instead of surrounding yourself with the white light you visualise the white light entering your body through the top of your head.

White-light visualisation can be used on a daily basis, helping you to feel balanced, calm and positive. If the energy is really toxic, like a psychic attack, I always use a dark blue cloak and a mirror ball to send the energy back to the source so the person can learn the karma.

I always close down my chakras after doing any type of work. You can do this easily by imagining your chakras like little lights winking out, one at a time.

I never worry about loved ones; I just place a white light around them daily and know they are always safe.

Grounding

Grounding is a therapeutic technique that involves certain activities that connect you to the earth. It can help you stay focused and retain information, is good for anxiety or stress, and has a calming effect, which is good for your emotional body. With any type of spiritual practice, the more grounded you are, the higher you can go as it helps you reconnect electrically to mother earth. Any type of exercise will do this, including gardening and walking, ideally for twenty or thirty minutes. It will also help you focus on your daily duties. Try pressing your hands into the grass or earth, lying on the grass, or hugging a tree. You can also immerse yourself in water; for instance, have an Epsom salt bath or go for a swim.

When working with any type of meditation or spiritual practice it's important to close down all your energy or you'll become scattered and ungrounded. I've seen this happen with a lot of healers and psychics. By staying open they lose focus in their lives, which become cluttered, and they find it impossible to organise themselves or finish things they've started.

To be successful with this work, grounding is an integral part of the journey. The more grounded you are, the higher you can go, and you can work in other dimensions and altered states quite easily.

BECOMING GROUNDED

1. Close your eyes, take a deep breath and imagine all your chakras as little lights.

2. Starting with the crown chakra, sweep energy down through all the chakras. Begin at the top of your head, and as you move take the energy down through the third eye, throat, heart, solar plexus, sacral and base, then deep into the earth.

3. Open your eyes.

Spiritual Healing

I first started to learn spiritual healing in the spiritualist churches I attended for many years. It was an incredible experience to see how we can tap into spirit energy. At the church, we would always do the healing in the middle of the service, before the medium of the day came on. We did the spirit presentation, bringing messages of love from the spirit world to the congregation.

Anyone in the congregation who wanted a healing on the day would indicate this by holding their hand in the air until one of the healers came to them. After a small prayer to invoke the energy, the healer would scan the person's aura with their hands and then begin to transfer energy by placing their hands in a certain area above the body, not touching the person. (This is not what is known as hands-on healing, which is another modality, or reiki, using symbols.) Like all types of healing, this practice, known as channelled energy, promotes self-healing in the person for mind, body and spirit.

The medium will usually start around the head area of the aura and work their way all around the body. The healing energy doesn't come from the medium, but from the universal or divine energy that is channelled through the medium or person giving the healing.

This healing energy can also be sent remotely, by first asking the person's higher self for permission, then visualising their body with warm glowing light, combined with feelings of love, compassion and healing. To add healing, the medium imagines them as healthy, happy and whole.

In my own healing sessions, which are done remotely these days, my aim as a healer is to clear and balance all the energy centres in the body, called chakras. Once I tune into the client and pick up information from their higher-self, guides and spiritual helpers, I then begin to clear lower-density vibrations in the auric field and send healing light into the chakras.

After I have finished and closed down both of us with protective energy and light, I may discuss how these vibrations were caused and give advice on how to stop them returning. At the end of the session, I will always convey the impressions I've picked up and encourage the client to take better care of themselves.

I have studied many types of healing throughout my work, including reiki, radiant healing, trance healing, reconnective healing, regression work and colour healing. I also use crystal healing and the use of symbols I've channelled, which I place in certain areas of the body to help with the healing process. When I first started healing, I did a lot of psychic surgery, where I would go into a trance state and become overshadowed by a healing guide.

Meditation

Meditation is the golden key to spiritual growth and spiritual development, as it connects you to your inner light, spiritual guides, soul groups, and your own higher self or eternal soul. Once you master this art, you'll discover the secrets to the inner wisdom you were born with and open a more empowering world. In simple words, you will, without doubt, be more aware and conscious of yourself, your surroundings, people, and nature and everything in it. You will also have peace of mind, as it will give you an opportunity to calm down to some degree.

Meditation teaches you to stop stressing, to ground, to focus, and to stop the kind of negative mind chatter that goes on in many people's heads on a daily basis. If not watched, negative mind chatter can attract negative people who are similar to the destructive energy you may be engaging with.

Everything you need in your life will be drawn to you and manifest easily. You just have to learn to surrender and go with the process. We are all energy, but vibrating on different frequencies.

By meditating for just twenty to thirty minutes a day you can bring so much peace into your life, and it will help to keep you younger because you'll be able to let go of the stresses and anxieties that life brings. The medical profession has proven that meditation is also a feasible practice for older adults and could offset age-related cognitive decline.

It is claimed that twenty minutes of meditation are equivalent to four hours of sleep on the theta level. It's a very important tool to help you on your spiritual journey, and in opening your awareness and connecting you with your higher self, angels, spirit helpers and your loved ones in spirit. Once you learn this easy process, your life will become more rewarding as it helps you go with the flow.

It's also a wonderful thing if you can teach meditation to your children.

CREATING A SACRED SPACE FOR MEDITATION

1. Creating a small, dedicated space in your home will make it easier for you to focus on meditation. Once you have set your mind on where that should be, the rest will be easy. Find a place you can call your own, where you feel safe and secure and where no one will interrupt you. The rewards will be so beneficial.

2. Once you have decided on your space, make sure you have a comfortable chair, bean bag or somewhere else nice to sit. Make sure the room is not cluttered and, if possible, open a window for fresh air. You could also spray the room with an energetic room and aura spray, which will help to get you in the mood.

3. Using a small table, create an altar with fresh flowers, candles, crystals, angels, statues or pictures that inspire you and set the mood.

4. Don't be surprised if your pets want to join in, as they will be attracted to the energy you have created in your sacred space. Allow them to do so as it's very healing for them as well, on so many levels. Our pets are our companion souls that come with unconditional love. They are here to help us and shower us with love. (If I don't let my cats in, they meow constantly until I open the door.)

5. It's important to sit up, as this aligns all your energy centres, or chakras. Also, if you lie down you might go to sleep, which means you won't be open to spirit messages. I once sat in a group with a woman who started to snore as soon as we went under into current. The teacher said it was because she needed healing. She told the woman to put white sheets on her bed when she got home and call in the spirit doctors to give her healing while she slept.

6. It's also important to meditate at the same time each day for better results when wanting to get messages from your guide or spirit helpers.

7. When you've finished your meditation for the day, always remember to close down all your chakras and send light, love and gratitude to the earth, animals, birds and everyone around you.

An Altar for Worship

An altar is a raised structure, table or spiritual tool that is used for prayer and worship. It's a focus point to help you work, for prayer, healing and manifestation in the world. It helps you focus for better outcomes, and can be used for protection, worship and manifesting your dreams and creative needs, and capturing what you love and need in your life through your intention. It's a very empowering exercise and a lot of fun because you're playing with positive energy and contacting your inner child.

With a bit of imagination, you can create an altar easily anywhere in your home. No matter how crowded your home is, you'll always find that special place for your time, the time that is yours alone. You can have one in an office, or a bedroom, where the energy will be calm, healing and restful. I have two in my own home, one is for myself and the other is for clients and world healing. For the healing altar, I always light a candle and say a prayer.

CREATING AN ALTAR

1. To set up a sacred space, use a small table, windowsill or a bench, and lay it with a white cloth and fresh flowers, pictures, statues, crystals, rocks, shells, feathers, icons, incense burner, candles, or whatever symbolises the divine source of all love to you. Take care not to create too much clutter by using too many things; be selective and mindful about what you choose.

2. You could take a walk in nature to collect some offerings for your rituals, things that you are drawn to, especially around the time of Earth's equinoxes, when natural energy shifts on the planet and there are celebrations of the changing season. When doing equinox rituals, it's good to use dried herbs such as rosemary, sage, chamomile, or incense such as sage, mirth or moss agate. You can place them on the altar, or around it. This creates a calm energy for everyone in the home to experience.

3. Now ask your angels and guides to join you as you create this special and beautiful work of art.

4. You could use incense or essential oils for a special aroma when you meditate. Some people like to do this, but it may not suit everyone. Harps and flutes also attract loving angels into your sacred space, but bells or any calm, relaxing music will do. I love to have seasonal fresh flowers on my altar, and pictures of my personal favourite masters or archangels, such as Jesus, Mother Mary, and the archangels Michael,

Raphael, Gabriel and Uriel, but it's up to you. We all come from different backgrounds and bring our own beliefs and practices.

Creating a Divine Space in Nature

For years I have had a nature space where I go when I need clarity in my life, as nature is so grounding and healing. If you create a similar space, it will help refresh and energise your spirit, and invigorate your body to embrace the beauty within.

When I was younger, after work I would head down to the beach, where all the worries of the day always disappeared as soon as I stepped out of the car. The warm sun on my back, the cool breeze in the air, and the smell of the salt from the sea in the back of my nose was always so refreshing; it washed over me in a cleansing way, as if washing all the stress and negativity from my body and from the long day.

These days I live very close to a large, busy city and next to a harbour where there are ancient trees that are hundreds of years old that give me so much pleasure, and are grounding and healing. When I walk past them, I can feel their incredible enormity and power.

In nature, we are connecting to the elemental kingdom with the sylphs, undines, salamanders and earth spirits that are connected to the trees and every other part of nature. If you don't have a similar place to go to, you can create a small space. Just sitting in your own garden will connect you to nature and the divine source, as the elementals work hand in hand with angelic energy.

MEDITATING IN YOUR SACRED SPACE

1. Sit down in your sacred space where you won't be disturbed, and imagine a column of vibrant white light washing over you. As you do this, feel it filling your entire being. As you breathe deeply, feel yourself going deeper and deeper, then anchoring your energy into the earth, where you will connect with the source of mother earth's pure energy of unconditional love.

2. Now, bring this energy back up to the base chakra until you feel it travelling through all the chakras, expanding everywhere throughout the cells of your body.

3. Now feel it gently rise above your head, higher and higher, going further and further into the ether all around you, until you feel as if you have reached the high point in the multiverse, which is unconditional love.

4. Once you have done this, expand your energy and awareness all around you, pushing it out as far as you can go. Allow yourself to let go of everything that no longer serves you. Surrender any trauma, anger, negativity or bad feelings towards yourself or others, and any fear or anxieties that may have been holding you back at this time. Imagine the darkness or blockages from all the cells in your body and mind being released into columns of light all around you.

5. Now slowly feel all your senses opening up, and if you hear anything in the background, like the sounds of nature or any other type of noise, use this to help you drift deeper and deeper. As you do this, imagine the warm gentle caress of the sun on your body, as if it's giving you energy for the day.

6. If you're having difficulty with mind chatter you can use a mantra like 'So Hum'; repeat this mantra in your mind as you slowly breathe in and out, and you will find it stopping your mind chatter.

7. When you're ready to come back, imagine closing down all your chakras, which look like tiny lights in your body, with a beam of light that goes all the way from the top of your head into the earth star, which is deep in the earth.

8. Now open your eyes slowly and see the new day. Don't be surprised at how much clearer and calmer you feel, and how everything looks so much brighter.

10

CONNECTING TO SPIRITS

Among the first things I learnt at the spiritualist church were what are called 'overheads', which means making a connection or link with a spirit in the spirit world when doing a reading for a loved one in the audience or congregation. (We're not working in the astral or wanting to make contact with earthbound souls.) Building up the energy for better communication is important as it blends the two worlds, and this can be helped by the congregation singing loudly. Once the songs are over, the medium stands on a platform or stage and brings through loved ones in spirit, with messages for the congregation.

Working as a medium is easy for me as I will always hear the spirit in question talking in my ear. I can hear the voice as though on the other end of a phone conversation. Others may have to rely on their other senses. Then, as the spirit comes closer, I will get a description in my mind's eye of what they looked like, how they died and what the connection was, plus names, places and a whole lot of information about what was going on in the loved one's life at the time.

Other times, I may see spirit people standing next to the client. With every reading, I also ask for something special that only the person connected would know, like a favourite song, or things they used to do together. I may mention a ring they're wearing on the day, or a piece of jewellery they may have received as a gift, or that was left as a token of love. This is known as validation, or evidence of survival, which the client always appreciates.

Once the link is made, I then start to get messages about the client to do with things that are going on in their lives. In the beginning of my training, this was scary, to say the least, but the more I relaxed and forgot about myself and everyone watching, the easier it was to read the congregation as spirit took over and helped me with my work. It also makes me feel good to know I will always have my guide and full spirit team working with me all the time.

It's important to know that spirit will always go to great lengths to get a message of love across to a loved one. The trouble is, not all spirits are good communicators, so the messages differ in length and quality, meaning that in some cases there may not be a lot of information. If this happens, I ask the spirit to come closer, encourage them to speak up, or ask them a question. If this doesn't work, it's time to move on to the next person as the spirit in question will usually be ready to move on also.

I once had a woman at a venue who refused to take the messages from her brother in spirit, who had hanged himself. The woman told me to stop and refused to say anything as the spirit man tried to connect with and talk to her. When this happened, I told the spirit man I was sorry and asked him to move on. I was then pulled in another direction by another spirit trying to make contact with a loved one.

If people are not open, I will close down the reading. If people are rude—if, for instance, they try to ridicule the medium, or behave disrespectfully in other ways—it's the medium's job to use discernment and not take it personally. Grief manifests in many ways, and there will always be non-believers who are out to get you if they can.

The information we get from loved ones in spirit includes names, how they died, what they looked like, what sort of life they lived, where they worked, foods they loved, and other information only the client will know. On the other hand, they may give a name, how they died, and just want to talk about what is going on in the receiver's life, which could be important.

People always ask me how the spirit knows what's going on in the receiver's life if they had never met them, or if they died when the person was young. Spirit people, believe it or not, know everything that's going on in our lives as they are connected to our love eternally, and will try to guide and help us in any way possible, just like our guardian angels.

Carol

Once I spoke to a woman in the audience named Carol, whose brother had been murdered. The angry spirit man, the brother, described how it happened and said he was upset that he'd been in the wrong place at the wrong time, and should never have become involved with such bad people. When he described how he had died, he said the police would catch the person or persons involved, because they were already aware of them.

> About three months later, Carol contacted me and said she felt happy because they had caught the man who shot her brother, just like her brother the spirit man had said. She was happy with the outcome, as her brother would now receive justice.

Not long after that I found myself working with a lot of murders, as spirit sometimes will work in themes. This time, while travelling around doing club shows, I brought through a woman in spirit who had been murdered by her husband, who was a suspect in the case. The trouble was, the police couldn't prove it. The spirit woman described how she had been strangled then dumped at sea, and said her husband had done it.

Her sister, the woman I was talking to in the audience, said she believed this to be true, as none of the family liked the husband's bullying ways. She said he was a creep and it was exactly what the family suspected. She also said that they knew in their hearts that her sister would not just disappear. She was a wonderful mother and close to her kids, and never in a million years would she ever want to leave them.

The weirdest thing about this night was to follow. There was a policewoman in the audience who apparently took an interest after listening to the reading. The spirit woman's sister rang me later and told me happily that the case was to be investigated further. Within three months the husband was convicted. According to the press, the police found evidence with the boat, which he still had covered in his yard.

It always amazes me to see the miraculous way spirit works, and in this case how this particular spirit woman had fought for justice.

11

WORKING WITH THE GENERAL PUBLIC

When I work with the general public, I always collaborate with my guide and spirit team, and ask that all the spirits wanting to come through line up so each can have their turn. It would be chaos otherwise, with all the spirits trying to jump in, and I would end up with confused messages. I then try to get through as many readings as I can.

Not everyone will get a reading on the day, because some spirits are better than others at jumping in, and some are excellent communicators. Sometimes I'll get what are called 'double links'—messages that are meant for more than one person. People will often come up and thank me afterward, saying they feel that they got a message, even though I didn't go to them.

After I have called the person's name from the spirit world and say how they died, people in the crowd will put up their hands. I normally know who is the right person to go to, because I'll feel an energy link, or pull. I've also worked by seeing a little light above a person's head when I've called out names. Other times I'll be drawn to somebody in the audience because I can see a spirit person standing next to them.

I make it a rule, before I do any work, to take the time to meditate, as I will always get a list of people's names to call out, which I write on a piece of paper on the day or night of the event.

I do two shows with a break in between when working in clubs, and during the break I'll leave the floor open and go to as many people as possible. The crowd is usually warmed up by then and the pace is faster. Occasionally, if I have a big audience, I'll blend my energy and work with another medium to get through as many people as possible. To be fair, I also try to give people the same amount of time and not spend ages on one particular person just because their spirit happens to be a good communicator.

When working with another medium, I prefer to take turns and not stand on the stage at the same time as them because of the spirit teams and piggy backing. This means I avoid tuning into the same client and giving similar information. I remember seeing new mediums in my earlier training doing this and feeding off the other medium's information and readings.

After I finish my work, I always close down all my chakras and centre myself back into my body. Then I have something to eat or drink. Some mediums I know like to have a cigarette or a drink, but I like to have a cup of tea when I get home to help relax me. I also watch a bit of late-night TV as I'm generally pumped and still buzzing from all the energy.

12

ANIMAL SPIRITS

Throughout my years as a psychic medium, I've served in many spiritualist churches, in my own office, and in different venues in clubs. All this work has helped me grow as a medium, and, as I have said many times, the audience and loyal clients will always support you in your work. Mediumship is, in my view, by far the greatest type of healing, as it proves time and time again that our loved ones are always with us, and that life as a soul is eternal. This includes what I call our companion souls, our beloved pets.

Often when I work, I'll see a bird fly across the room, or an animal run in and sit quietly next to someone in the audience. I've seen dogs, cats, birds and horses that have all crossed over to spirit. I've been asked more than once by clients if I could find out how their beloved pet is doing and if they can give me confirmation that their pet is safe. I've also worked with animals or pets with spiritual healing, as they too have a chakra system.

Years ago, at a spirit and psychic venue, I saw the spirit of a beautiful little white poodle sitting next to an elderly lady in the audience. The dear little thing was sitting quietly, not really paying me any attention, occasionally looking up as it cleaned itself, and staying aloof. Walking over to the lady, I started to tune in to the little spirit dog. As I described what I saw to the woman, she became confused, saying the dog wasn't hers.

Normally I would have closed down the reading and moved on, but my guide told me to persevere; there was a message for the woman that she needed to hear to help her move on in the healing process. After what seemed like a long pause, the woman suddenly started sobbing, as if she'd been holding in her emotions for a long time.

Then, looking up, she wiped her eyes and said she couldn't believe it. It was indeed her little companion, but she didn't think it possible that animals could make a spirit connection and come through. She told me that the little poodle was her beloved little Peppy, who had died a few months before. She was very upset. She said she had never had the experience of seeing a medium before, so it had shocked her. She pulled something out of her bag. Overwhelmed, she stood up proudly and showed everyone in the room Peppy's collar and a toy trinket she had kept as a keepsake.

Another time, in a club this time, I saw a beautiful chestnut horse with a brown star on its head standing next to a man in the audience. As I went to him, I described what I could see. Startled, he said he was a jockey, and the horse I was seeing was his old racehorse and best friend. As I spoke to the horse, the message was that the man's wife was pregnant and it was a boy. When I relayed this to the man and his partner, they looked shocked. After a few seconds they said it was supposed to be a secret, and yes, it was correct.

What should have been a joyful occasion turned weird later on. The man's parents, who were sitting next to him and his wife, were not impressed. They had not been told about the pregnancy. After the show had finished, they marched up to me and said they didn't think it was right that their son's horse should be the one to spill the beans, so to speak. Luckily for me, the audience loved the message. I was only doing my job, passing on all the spirit messages.

Another time, when I took my mother to a spirit show, I brought many birds and animals through with the readings. On the way home in the car, my mother sat in stony silence. When I asked her if she'd liked the show, she turned to me angrily and said, 'Animals don't talk. It was all rubbish.'

It always amazes me to see how people have such fixed ideas, and cannot appreciate the concept that anything is possible with spirit.

13

PSYCHOMETRY

Psychometry, also known as readings, was once used as a tool to predict the future, rather like reading tea leaves or coffee cups, and using tarot cards. The practice is very similar to scrying, which I described in detail in an earlier chapter. Psychometry is a psychic way of seeing or reading something that isn't typically visible. In the classroom, psychometry is a great skill for beginners to use to get psychic links or imprints because it's really quite easy to do. Psychometry, also known as token-object reading, can be used for missing people, as they provide good links. It's also used in murder cases.

Like everything in life, the more you practise your psychometric skills, the easier and quicker it will become for you. To do psychometry, you should remember to have fun, relax, and not stress yourself over it.

Flower Readings

Flower psychometry, or reading, was a form of earth magic that originated in ancient times and was used by healer priests and shamans. Later in history, it was applied by Celtic tribes, which used all sorts of plants and flowers in prediction rituals and customs such as foreseeing a person's fortune with regard to love, health or wealth.

Flowers have long been used to communicate messages, but there is also a history of folklore using flowers for inner communication and divination. Other parts of flower psychometry have been passed down through the generations by traveling Romany people, who still sell posies of wildflowers and herbs, and who still use flowers for fortune-telling.

Flowers are powerful and have a very strong life force, which is very healing, visually, physically and emotionally. It's no wonder they're used therapeutically in vibrational therapy as essences, which I have used in my practice for years, not only for myself and family but also for clients.

When used in readings, flowers are an excellent tool and a good conduit of energy when aligned with our higher selves; they operate so easily for the opening up of mediumship abilities. Flowers are wonderful messengers from spirit for mediums and psychics who are just beginning.

I first started reading flowers in the spiritualist church, where I saw many mediums work as part of their development. In the beginning I found it very helpful for psychic links, but as I quickly advanced, I found I could no longer work with flowers in this way. Instead, I put the flowers down once I made contact with the spirit around the person, and was able to go on with the mediumship reading as all the information was there.

HOW TO READ FLOWERS

1. Before the meeting starts, everyone places a flower they have brought from home in a paper bag in a basket in the room. No one can see anyone else's flower.

2. The basket is passed around the room and everyone is invited to take a bag.

3. One at a time, each person takes the flower from their bag, opening up all their senses: sight, smell, taste, feelings and touch. They then share their impressions of the person who brought it going by what they can feel on the flower.

4. Once everyone has done this, they all put the flowers down. Ask if there is any spirit around them that wants to get a message of love across, asking the usual questions to do with mediumship, and encouraging them to come closer.

5. Once the messages are all gone, close down. Always close down after a session, ground, and sweep white light through your energy centres.

Jewellery Readings

Like all readings, this should always be done with the client's permission. When we're working with pieces of personal items or crystals, the information we're getting comes from the energetic psychic imprint, which we all have. Examples of objects to read are watches, wallets, phones, rings and other items the client wore or wears a lot, and which have been on their body. This can be for someone living, missing people, and people that have passed.

For information regarding missing or deceased animals, pets or birds, a collar or any other item the animal once used can be used to get a good connection, or link. All living beings have a life force and an energetic vibration.

Because of the metal content, I prefer to work with larger pieces like a watch for a psychic link for information about a person, place or situation, because these items have a large amount of residual energy compared to pieces of clothing or tiny objects.

HOW TO READ JEWELLERY

1. Before a reading, wash your hands and place protective energy around yourself. Then open yourself up, asking for guidance with your ritual or prayer.

2. As you hold the object, keep your eyes open, not closed. You will begin to get images in your mind's eye, like a movie. Open up all your senses: hearing, sight, touch, smell, taste, and psychic senses.

3. Once you've done this, you should be able to get a very comprehensive psychic reading of what is going on in the person's life—past, present and future—with good and helpful information about the person. When working with a missing person, I'm often asked if they're still alive, or where they are. If I don't hear a voice when I call out 'Is anyone there?' this is a good omen; it means they're still alive.

4. Ask the spirit to show you a picture of where they are, and you'll usually get an image of this in your mind, or the name of a place.

5. As you hold the object for a link and receive psychic impressions, ask the spirit to come closer, and talk to them if possible. When you've finished, send the spirit off to the spirit world with your spirit team, with love and blessings.

6. Always close down after a session and sweep white light through your energy centres. If needed, the session can be recorded.

Picture Readings

In mediumship readings I will often use a picture of the person to read as a psychic link, which can give me a lot of impressions and then a direct communication. Spirit will always teach us things all the time on our journey.

Years ago, while travelling in Barcelona, I was looking at a famous painting in the foyer of an art gallery. Suddenly I heard a voice talking in my ear and, confused, I looked around to see where the voice was coming from. I realised that I was alone, and it was in fact the painter of the artwork talking to me telepathically. I just let go, knowing that anything is possible when working in the spirit world. I took a deep breath, silenced my mind and listened to what the spirit man had to say.

He told me about his time on Earth, which included the politics of his time, the art, the food, and how important it was for his legacy to make a statement with his art. After he finished speaking, I made my way outside and sat down for a while with my thoughts, wondering how it was possible. The other strange thing was that when this happened, the foyer of the art gallery was empty, when normally there would be hundreds of people walking around.

This is what I call 'spirit intervention', another lesson to learn from the spirit world about what is possible to use with spirit connections. When I told my husband my strange experience, he just laughed and said, 'Nothing surprises me with you.'

When we returned to the hotel, I found a picture of the artist online, which confirmed that he was the artist who had created the painting I had been looking at. Everything he had said was correct.

If asked, I will sometimes use photographs in my private sittings and with audiences, as they can be quite successful in getting a direct link. Mediums are often able to link into the spirit person, hear their voice, and receive messages. Once the link is made, the spirit generally stands by the medium and gives the information, which the medium relays to the person, and puts the photograph down.

I have also taught this in my classes with a lot of success, and I encourage people who have lost loved ones to talk to the loved one's photo, as the spirit in question will always hear them, no matter what they think. Another way to practise and improve your skills is to 'read' pictures in magazines, but don't talk about it with other people, as a mark of respect. Over time you will be able to improve your psychic skills as you master this gift.

HOW TO READ PICTURES

1. As you open up, relax and feel the back of the picture in front of you. As you do this, turn the photo around and tune your energies in to it.

2. Once you're focused, look at the face of the person and connect yourself, mind-to-mind, with the energy of the person. If you can't see clearly, use a magnifying glass and make sure you have good light. Eventually the photo will give you a psychic link and you'll receive clear impressions, information and messages from the person, which can sometimes manifest as a voice in your head.

3. As you concentrate further, you may eventually sense the spirit in the room and begin communication. Generally, the person in the group who is related to the deceased person can clarify whether you were right or wrong.

4. Once you finish relaying the entire message, close yourself down. Always close down after a session and sweep white light through your energy centres.

I have used this technique with pets and been able to have long dialogues with them. When a pet has come through, other spirit people related to the client will often come into the room.

This process can also be used to detect illness in healings. To do this, scan your hand chakras, which are in the middle of your palm, over the photo. You will receive hot and cold impressions.

Pendulum Readings

Many people enjoy working with a pendulum to make communication with a spirit, to help find lost objects, detect the location of missing persons, and clear chakras, to name a few useful things. With clearing chakras, the pendulum is placed over each energy centre, one at a time, starting with the base energy centre. The pendulum will spin right then left by itself. Once this is completed, the chakra is clear.

One of the first things to do is to discover how you, and your higher self, like to communicate with your pendulum. For example, when you ask it what is a *yes*, it may swing to the left; ask it again what is a *no* and it may swing to the right. Test the answers by asking something you know the answer to. Once you know how to receive the *yes* and *no* answers, the process of using a pendulum can begin. Using a pendulum is really quite simple and may vary according to the different types of crystals you're drawn to. I always preferred clear quartz in my early days, but I no longer use them as I get simple answers by asking yes or no questions to my guide, who stands on my left side.

When you have confidence, you can go further and ask things you don't know but want to know. The pendulum can be used in working out answers to all sorts of things. Understand that this is an effective tool and is not to be misused, abused or used repeatedly. Avoid using it to play games, for instance, like asking: *Does he love me? Will I ever find love? When will I die?* and so on.

HOW TO READ A PENDULUM

1. Find a quiet place for meditation where you won't be disturbed. Now open up all your senses, asking them to work for your highest good.

2. Place your pendulum in front of you and sweep it with white light to clear it. Do this each time you use it.

3. Now ask it a question: Which side is *yes*, and which side is *no?* Write down the answers on a piece of paper.

4. For missing persons, when you're looking for a location, place your pendulum over a map. When it starts to spin by itself, you have your location. You can test this a few times, and ask others you're working with to have a go as well for clarification.

5. When you've finished, close down by sweeping white light through your energy centres, or chakras.

14

CRYSTALS FOR AWARENESS

Crystals can be used for support, to improve awareness, and for psychic growth. I've always loved the magic energy of crystals as they're conduits for and amplifiers of subtle and incredible energy. Through past lives and deep meditations, I've seen myself back in Atlantis in ancient times, working as a priestess in temples with people lying on big slabs of clear-quartz crystals, which were healing beds. I still remember the heat they emitted.

These days I love to wear them on my body for protection, as talismans to draw positive experiences into my life, such as love, friendships and abundance in work. I also use them decoratively, as it feels so good to have them around.

They need to be cleansed, as they can store a lot of negative energy you may pick up along the way. If the stone allows—they all have different qualities—you could put it in a bath with a little lavender oil, smoke it with sage, or let it sit under a full moon.

When I worked at festivals with other readers, at the end of the table I kept a wand with a clear-quartz crystal, which was programmed for protection, and to stop psychic attack and the negative energy that was often thrown around by jealous and inferior readers. I had to do this as it was getting too hard to find assistants to work the day with me, as the energy was often so shamefully toxic that they would complain of feeling sick or drained, or getting terrible headaches for no reason. It was amazing how well the wand worked, and I never had any problems with my assistants after that. It created an energy bubble of protection.

One dreadful woman I knew walked around jabbing fingers in people's faces, telling them they were cursed. I've heard through the grapevine that this woman is still struggling, is very lonely and has health issues, which is not surprising because any negative energy you throw out always comes back tenfold; this is the law of karma. How these types stay in the industry is beyond me.

Types of Crystals

Moldavite

This unique, cosmic gemstone is said to be of extra-terrestrial origin, created as the result of a meteorite crash that occurred millions of years ago. It's known to be a stone to serve the inhabitants of this planet, a quantum-leaps stone, helping you rapidly shift your vibration and life circumstances.

Moldavite in its simplest form stimulates cooperation between those of extra-terrestrial origins and those who are experiencing life on Earth. It holds immense potential for direct interdimensional accessing of higher dimensional galactic energies, to draw into the Earth plane those thought patterns and light vibrations that are optimal for one's preparation for ascension and illumination.

It attracts high frequencies of light that activate and clear all chakras and the energy field, especially the throat, the third and crown chakra used for channelling. It's known to bring in new connections, bright opportunities, and a positive flow that is true to your designated soul's purpose and mission, if you chose to take this path on Earth, as it activates all your chakras. It also lifts all your senses to a higher frequency and helps you remember your star origins.

Moldavite is best used with celestite, aquamarine, diamond, lapis, opal, black diopside, moss agate, and smoky quartz, to name a few. It also works well with quartz, which adds the factors of amplification and stabilisation of the moldavite stone.

Please note that it's a very powerful stone that some people might not be able to handle. I had a large piece of this stone, but it disappeared when I moved. This happens a lot when crystals are no longer required to work with you; they will sometimes move to somebody else who needs them more.

Blue apatite

I call this beautiful stone, which has a lovely colour, the regal stone. One was given to me early on in my career, when I worked in a crystal shop. I've since passed it on to one of my students, who sat with me for years. A potentially brilliant young psychic, I felt she needed it to help her improve her abilities; I believed she needed the energies the stone had to offer to take her to another level.

Blue apatite is known as the stone of psychic activation and cosmic connection. It releases debris in the aura and opens the way for mediumship and psychic abilities such as clairaudience, clairvoyance, clairolfaction, clairsentience and channelling.

Labradorite

This is the healing stone used for psychic and spiritual people who do healing work for themselves and the collective. I used to love to call this stone the 'angel crystal', as it reminds me of feeling as if you're being pulled into another reality—another galaxy, parallel universe or dimension—that is much lighter than our own heavy and dense planet.

I now call it the 'psychic's stone', as energetically it's very powerful. It's possible to feel and imagine the other dimension and doors it offers as you're pulled by its energy while it facilitates the transformation of intuition into intellectual thought.

It's a good stone to have on your desk. It also protects the aura, or energy field, as it helps to keep the aura clear, balanced, protected and free from energy leaks. It assists in the alignment of the subtle bodies, enhancing the connection between the physical and ethereal realms. Labradorite is said to represent 'the temple of the stars', helping you sustain and maintain while providing for the understanding of the destiny you have chosen.

When I first started working in crystal shops and New Age stores as a reader, one of my managers gave me a labradorite ring that I still have today. She believed that the stone was meant for me since it works on so many levels, including telepathy, astral travel, prophecy, psychic reading, access to the Akashic records, past-life recall, and communication with spirit helpers. As mentioned, crystals have a tendency to move on once they've finished their contract with you, but this ring has stayed with me for many years while I've been working as a medium and reader.

I highly recommend this stone, as it opens up your higher self, channel, chakras, energy field and higher wisdom, and can be used in so many tangible ways as it connects to your energy system.

Lapis Lazuli

Lapis lazuli is divine and is, of course, another one of my favourite stones. When I wear it on my skin, I can feel my third eye opening up ever so gently. Among crystal lovers, this stone is known fondly as the 'wisdom stone', as it has a mystical appearance, and increases and empowers the psychic senses.

Not only is it a protective stone, it's also used to encourage self, morality, awareness, self- confidence, ancient wisdom stored in an individual's DNA or blueprint, compassion, love and harmony, and increases latent psychic abilities. It's also very good for protection against psychic attacks, depression and emotional anxiety, as it encourages deep harmony, inner truth, self-awareness and self-expression.

In healing, its properties clear the throat, cool and soothe inflammation, reduce insomnia, and help overcome depression and vertigo. It's also a helpful tool for creating new ideas, releasing anger, calming the mind, and opening the third eye. It's a beautiful, celestial deep-blue stone, consisting of blue lazurite, sparkling pyrite, cloudy white calcite and other minerals. Historically, it was used throughout the ages by ancient Egyptians, Babylonians, Minoans, Greeks, and the Chinese and Romans. It's also known to be connected to heavenly energies.

I like to keep a piece on my body, as this stone speaks to the wearer when they need it, making them fearless and motivated, and helps them ground and focus.

Aquamarine

Aquamarine is known as the 'stone of courage', as its qualities are known to enhance the capacity for rapid intellectual response, and to access the assimilation of inner knowledge as it quickens the process and helps with learning. It also provides a shielding property for the aura and subtle bodies, thus is a favourite for sensitive souls and empaths to prepare for difficult and trying times.

It also works with the alignment of the chakras, and balancing the network of structures connecting the physical and ethereal bodies. As it enhances the connection to the higher-self or soul energy, helping us go deeply into ourselves, it assists in attuning to more spiritual bodies of awareness for those sensitive souls who are involved, or want to be involved, with spiritual studies and development.

Aquamarine also helps with the throat chakra, helping us voice our thoughts and ideas, take personal responsibility for our actions, and clearly communicate our wants and needs.

It's no wonder that healers are attracted to this precious stone. It's one of my favourite stones, especially in the raw form, and it reminds me of a planet scientists refer to as 'water world', which is not in our own universe and star system, but far away in another galaxy. I have had a past life on this very calming planet, and because of those memories, aquamarine's colour and healing support me unconditionally.

15

CRYSTAL GRIDS

I love to play with crystals because they are good amplifiers of energy, and I especially love placing them around my home in different sections of the space, for example, the far-left section of the house away from the front door, which is called the prosperity section. I have a large amethyst crystal there, as it's good for dissolving negativity. In the far right, which is the relationship section, I have a beautiful large rose quartz, which enhances love and creates harmony in all my relationships.

Home crystal grids can be created to help you in any area of your life; the power of the crystals amplifies the energy that can help with increasing abundance, cleansing spaces, healing and love, attracting angels, mastering energies you want to work with, and creating an ambient space and relaxing atmosphere. It's a creative way to manifest all your dreams, goals and intentions.

Crystal grids can also be used with the intention of protecting your home and work, and can be used with meditation. By combining all the different stones, each with their own unique energies, you can make all types of grids. A crystal grid is not only a tool, but a special arrangement of beautiful healing stones to attract your dreams and outcomes.

You usually start with a main crystal in the middle that is larger than the rest, then arrange smaller stones in some type of pattern encircling the centre stone. With whatever intention you have, you place the stones on the altar, which is generally in a place for meditation, or wherever else you believe will give you the desired result. If the crystals become dusty, you need to clean them or they will not work.

Once I have created my grid for whatever intention, I use a wand with a clear-quartz point to give the stones energy. I point the wand at each crystal with the intention I desire for my outcome.

For crystal layouts on a client's body, I like to place a crystal that represents the chakra or energy centre of the body directly on top. At the client's feet I place a grounding healing stone, and at the crown chakra on the top of the head I place clear quartz, with the point towards the head. There are many ancient ways to play with crystal layouts on the body, and when you learn to do this with a good teacher you will find your hands-on spiritual healing or reiki work will improve. Crystals have amazing properties, are conductors of energy, and without doubt will enhance a healing or massage.

Crystal grids are often referred to as 'the energetic marriage of sacred geometry', with our dearest crystals used with the intention of making our dreams, desires, intentions and goals a reality.

Sacred geometry is all around us. It is in nature—in forests, trees, leaves and branches—and in spiral galaxies, and the cells of the human body. Many believe sacred geometry provides the container for all of life. Through the study of sacred geometry, we can gain an understanding of the universe around us and unlock the building blocks of creation.

Under a microscope, crystals look like they have repeating patterns of sacred geometrical formations. When we make a crystal grid, we are aligning the appropriate stones and geometric form with our intentions to manifest.

The Central Stone

Setting up a crystal grid is about tuning into your own power or intuition. There are no rules. You will be led by your own intuition, and your feelings of what you want, which is very empowering. Most crystal grids include a central stone, surrounding stones, and amplification stones, like small clear-quartz crystals. Once cleared, you can program all your stones by running them under water, smoking them with some sage, then giving them a command.

The centre stone, or torus, acts like an anchor for the grid's energy; it can also be thought of as an antenna that broadcasts your intentions into the universe. The centre stone is always the largest stone on your energy grid and all the other crystals are placed around it. I also like to place my energy grid on a white clean cloth, then small candles around the grid, and I sometimes use a statue of an archangel as an extra bonus when I've finished.

Since this is your grid, how you create it is completely up to you. Once you've set up the grid, on a piece of paper write down exactly what you need in your life and place it under the torus, or central stone.

The crystals that you arrange around the central stone are usually tumbler stones. You can use as many as you like; again, it's up to you. These stones act as modifiers in your grid, like small satellites receiving and broadcasting your intentions out into the world.

Amplification stones are optional. They are quartz points or tumbles placed in geometric points between the surrounding stones. These will power up your grid.

Activating Your Crystal Grid

This is the most important thing to do, especially when working with crystals. You can use a crystal wand, a pendulum, or a tuning fork that you use to create a sound by hitting a piece of quartz, then placing it over the crystals in your grid.

When you're ready to activate your crystals, you need to have a clear and concise statement in your mind of what it is you want to manifest in your life. Say this aloud in a clear voice, repeating it three times as you activate your centre crystal first with your hand or tool, visualising pure energy entering the crystal.

Once you've done this, next activate the other crystals, from the inside out, until you feel you've finished. When completed, thank the devas of the crystals for their help and assistance, and place white light around your energy grid.

Crystal grids can also be used for protection, to bring in positive energy while meditating or in a trance, so you feel safe from outside influences when doing your own work. You can also create a crystal altar to attract love into your life. This is a lot of fun, is easy to do and, although simple, it is effective, as all healing works with intention. Why be lonely when you have the power to attract love into your life with simple and easy-to-do magic?

CREATING A CRYSTAL ALTAR

1. Find a small table or bench to work with. Lay out a white cloth and decorate it with all the crystals you want to work with.

2. If your grid is for love, protection or success with your work, place a large piece of selenite as an anchor for energy in the middle of the table.

3. Place six clear-quartz crystals in a circle around the central stone to enhance its energy.

4. Lay a circle of six rose-quartz crystals for unconditional love.

5. On the very outside, place six blue kyanite crystals for protection.

6. Underneath the central stone, place a piece of paper with your desired outcome written on it, including as many details as possible. You may also like to place a few small candles on the energy grid when meditating. I like to spray my grid with an aromatherapy spray, such as lavender. Anything that smells good for the senses will do.

7. Now you need to program your crystals on your energy grid by using a tuning fork with a large quartz crystal, a clear-crystal wand or a pendulum, making your wishes and intentions very clear. Clear tumblers of quartz crystals are great conduits of energy, and are easy to use and program. Rose quartz and blue kyanite have powerful qualities as well.

8. There are many grids you can create for so many things, but be careful not to have your layout too cluttered, and never allow it to become dusty as that will stop it from working or being effective. The key thing is to make sure you program each crystal for more effectiveness.

16

CRYSTAL SINGING BOWLS

Having a background in music, I've always been interested in vibrational-sound therapy. This therapy retunes your body, mind and spirit, encouraging relaxation, healing and a balanced and therapeutic wellness. The combination of tones and vibrations can be played with bowls sitting on the body, on a table, or on the ground in front of you and the client. The whole process creates a state of relaxation and pure indulgence as the sounds act as a total massage for the nervous system.

The importance of sound therapy in healing work has been well known and documented for generations. The first time I heard the sound of the crystal singing bowls I felt my heart sing, and I had a smile on my face for days afterward.

These unique bowls are made of pure quartz, and are used to rebalance and cleanse all your chakras. They can be clear, or in the colours of the different chakras they represent. The clear-quartz singing bowls contain seven rainbow colours, which stimulate seven energy centres, or chakras, of the body, and a musical octave.

Sound healing, or sound therapy, has been practised since ancient times. It's like vibrational flower remedies that are used as essences, and is based on the idea that everything in the universe, including our bodies, is in a state of vibration because of its crystalline structure.

Like any type of healing, sound can unblock energy through soundwaves, which bring harmony through oscillation and resonance, helping restore the body's natural balance from disease mentally, psychically, emotionally and spiritually. This therapy is believed to transmit energy to the aura, affecting the brain and resulting in an improved state of consciousness.

The musical notes for each chakra:

- Base chakra: red, C
- Naval: orange, D
- Solar plexus: yellow, E
- Heart: green, F
- Throat: blue, G
- Third eye: indigo, A
- Crown: violet, B
- Transpersonal point: purple, B#

When I first began to collect my set of singing bowls, I decided I would have a kind of initiation to welcome them into the world. I was very appreciative of their sound and couldn't wait to experience more learning and healing from the sound frequencies.

I started with cleansing them by placing them in a warm bath with a tiny sprinkling of lavender oil to release any residual energy. I then placed them gently on a towel outside, with not too much sun, to dry slowly. When they were dry, I picked up one bowl at a time with the intention of placing my own psychic imprint on them. I asked the crystal energy of the bowl to work in harmony with me for healing.

When they travelled with me, I used supportive containers for each bowl to protect them. Whenever I worked with them, I would imagine clearing them with white light a few times, or smoking them to clear any residual energy. With my set of singing bowls, over the years I have played at commitment ceremonies, and I even played at my daughter's first marriage by the sea. Placing all my bowls on a flat surface or a table, I played them with my mallet, starting from the base and making my way up to the higher energy centres, then I improvised, depending on the mood. Everyone loved the calming sound and thanked me afterward.

When I ran meditation classes and introductions for trance, I always used the bowls to help take the students into a very deep state, which they totally loved. Singing bowls can take you to a whole other level of bliss and incredible insight.

I even made a track with another musician for space clearing the home or place of business using drums and percussion. This is still free to listen to today on YouTube.

We are all different, and some people are not able to handle the noise and frequency of the bowls, finding it overpowering and irritating. Once, while playing the bowls, a very rude woman, a professional singer, came up after the session and told me I was trying to destroy her singing voice. She claimed that each time I hit, or played, the throat-chakra bowl, it gave her great pain. I have to say I received a shock as I have never had such a bad experience before when working with the singing bowls.

Feeling disappointed, I told her how sorry I was, as this was not my intention, and suggested she should see a throat specialist as she may have had a blockage or nodule which the bowl was picking up on, as the bowls are designed to clear blocked energy in the body for healing. Unimpressed, she walked away, scolding and swearing under her breath, as if I had attacked her in some way.

Saddened by this, and disappointed, I spoke to the bride at a later date and told her what had happened. She said she wasn't surprised as the woman had been working overseas and was very stressed. While on tour, she had had a heavy work schedule and was forced to cancel her concerts because of her throat. Perhaps she should have realised the bowls were only warning her of a much larger problem she needed to address and was already aware of.

It certainly is interesting how some people will often, subconsciously, project their problems onto others because of their own frustration, anger and ignorance. These bowls are nothing but joy to so many others, and have proved to me time and time again how important sound therapy is in our lives, therapeutically. At the time, I said a prayer for the woman and asked spirit to guide her to a good doctor.

17

LIGHT AND DARK ENERGIES

Everything in the universe, including planet Earth and, importantly, us, is made up of pure energy. We, and everyone around us and in our lives, also transmute energy. One way to look at it is to think of us as small transmitters, like telegraph poles with signals, and others who have the same frequency or vibration as us will be attracted by our energy.

But not everyone is love and light in our world. If you're a person who is happy and contented with your life, you will attract others who are the same and who will want to help you. If, on the other hand, you are negative, ego based, wanting power, or are nasty or vindictive, you will always seem to draw bad experiences or negative energy towards you. This is the universal law: what you give out comes back to you tenfold.

There are also two types of energy that people work with, and these energies do not blend:

- Light energy: This energy is universal love. It's the strongest energy in our world and is nothing but unconditional, loving, healing and powerful. It's the most powerful energy in the universe as it's unconditional. People who work with this energy are called lightworkers.

- Dark/negative energy: This energy is thicker, often sticky, and is extremely manipulative. It works faster than white energy, but it's extremely malevolent. There can be repercussions with this energy. For example, people who use this energy and work with the dark arts, or this type of evil and dark energy, may be successful for a while, but will suffer emotionally in the long term. They will never feel fully loved in their personal relationships, will suffer blockages, often get sick, and are likely to have constant money problems. I've met many people of this type and it often confuses me initially because they can come across as poor-me types, but over time they will always suck other people's energy and use their resources.

Benny

A couple of years ago, Benny, a young student in my group, didn't have the courtesy to turn up regularly, and did not have the focus to learn the lessons I was teaching. He was always distracted. When he first sat in my group, he claimed to be an energy healer and said he had worked in healing centres.

I was fascinated by his stories and loved hearing about his healing, which he said had been passed down to him by his grandmother, who was what he called a 'wise woman' in her country. He sounded so proud of his heritage and he was constantly saying how much his grandmother had taught him about all sorts of things, even spell craft, but it was easy to see he was all talk.

When I questioned him more closely, he either didn't answer or gave vague replies.

It didn't take too long for me to see that Benny was a time waster and had no intention of ever contributing or learning anything. In fact, over time he used the group as a counselling session to talk about his miserable life and all his problems, demanding to be heard and not giving others a chance to speak. In the long run, his true colours were shown. To me, this was another lesson in boundaries and trying to rescue others.

Benny complained about how he had been kicked out of the healing centre he was working at when I first met him. He was very angry and said he had been used and abused by the owner, claiming that he did most of the work and was practically running the centre. He was also furious that the woman he complained about was also taking half his money, and as far as he was concerned, that wasn't fair.

Once I got the vibe that something wasn't right, I ran out of patience. I told him I couldn't help him anymore and asked him to leave. Then I cut all ties; I excluded his energy from the group's oversoul, releasing his residual energy. I also removed from my office the gifts of strange little dolls that I had received from him weekly, which I felt were constantly watching me. They had a strange, unpleasant energy as well, which made me feel very anxious.

Not long after, I got confirmation that my fears had been right. One of my other students rang in tears, telling me

> that Benny had been phoning her constantly and saying horrible things about me and the rest of the group.
>
> A few months later I heard that he had been trying to take me down by spreading false rumours. It never affected my work, though, as I was always invited back. I guessed that everyone eventually worked him out for themselves.

Often when I'm clearing negative energy, lost spirits or dark energies from clients' homes or land, and smoking out spaces, I will find this energy hard to work with. As it's not light energy, it's impossible to send it into a column or porthole of light, so I will send it back to the earth, or wherever it came from. It's easier to send it back to Mother Nature, with the help of my spirit team and the nature spirits from the elemental kingdom.

The type of negative energy I'm talking about is not very nice. It's very draining, and in some cases is associated with murders and assaults, or any type of indecent acts that have occurred in that vicinity.

> ## Rosie
>
> Rosie and I were friends as teenagers. She was older than me, but had an uncanny knack of getting involved with the wrong type of man, who would use and abuse her as she was, sadly, a hopeless romantic. I don't know how many times I tried to rescue her, or give her advice, but she never listened to me and carried on, going from one toxic relationship to the next.

Every time she came to my house, she would pester me non-stop to read her cards, always asking if her latest boyfriend was 'the one'. It was always the same. She would be swept off her feet and the romance would progress very quickly, but before long she would be dumped and end up in the same cycle of abuse.

Whenever I suggested anything positive, such as taking time to get to know someone instead of jumping straight into bed, she would stubbornly shake her head, not listening, and change the subject.

I was way out of my depth as I was just a teenager myself, but one thing I did know was that Rosie was an energy vampire, someone who drained me every time I tried to help her. My mother, who has aways had a good sense of people's characters, never liked her or had any tolerance for her. Trying not to laugh, I would watch in silence as Mum rolled her eyes when Rosie told the same story over and over again. Each time, we both knew the relationship would not end in a good way.

Rosie was sure that Ivan was the one. Not only was he good in bed, but he was also spiritual and knew a lot about magic. When she told me he was into magic, I gave in and agreed to meet him, against my better judgement. Before we left, I did a quick spread with the tarot, which confirmed my fears. I saw the devil card, the tower and the three of hearts, which meant Ivan was not a good person. There would be trouble and Rosie would end up heartbroken and in tears. I told her this, but she didn't listen.

When we arrived at Ivan's house, I had a bad feeling immediately. The old home looked unloved, lonely and isolated, as if nobody had lived there for a long time. From the road, it looked desolate, but it was well hidden from prying eyes. As we made our way through the front yard, which was overgrown with weeds, thorns, scrubs and old twisted trees, I noticed that all the windows were tightly shut and the shutters had been pulled down. The closer we got to the front door, the more I felt that something was horribly wrong. I got goosebumps all over my body, my throat felt dry, I felt weak at the knees and I began to sweat profusely.

It didn't get any better when we went inside. The house was dirty and dark, and I was berating myself for agreeing to come. It all felt wrong. Rosie walked through the house, calling his name. He wasn't there. Rosie was disappointed but I was relieved. I continued to follow her, slowly, and I began to burp softly, which was an indication the energy was bad.

We reached a locked room at the end of a hallway. Rosie became excited, and wanted me to see inside. As soon as we unlocked the door and stepped inside the darkened room, I was hit by a terrible smell that made me want to vomit. The air was putrid, as though a dead creature had rotted away in a corner. I covered my mouth and nose, trying not to breathe too deeply.

Stumbling around in the dark, I yelled at Rosie to put the light on and was suddenly overwhelmed by an ice-cold chill. Whatever was going on, it wasn't good, but I was determined to find out what it was.

A thick dusty red velvet curtain was covering something huge in the middle of the room. I pulled at the velvet material and got the shock of my life when it fell off. Under it was a life-sized female mannequin dressed in an ancient-style robe. Dried blood appeared to have run down from its mouth and it held a dagger in its hand, which was also covered in dried blood.

I also saw what looked like an altar full of dirty bottles, sharp knives and half-burnt candles, and hundreds of used matches lay scattered across the floor. Statues of dark, demonic creatures had been placed carefully throughout the room, as though part of some kind of weird ritual.

Going by the stench and amount of dried blood everywhere, plus the fur, bones and skulls littering the room, it appeared that animals and birds had been sacrificed—slaughtered and cut up into tiny pieces that were now covered in flies.

I took a deep breath and, regaining my composure, glared at Rosie, furious that she had gotten herself involved in something so evil. She was standing meekly beside me, not saying a word, just staring at me stupidly with a puzzled expression on her face.

I was furious. I asked her why she couldn't see what Ivan was into, and why she had involved me. Couldn't she see that this was totally wrong?

'You don't understand,' she said. 'Ivan's a master magician. He's even asked me to go with him to the cemetery next time to collect more old bones and things for his altar.'

The drive home seemed to take forever. We both sat without speaking, listening to loud rock music on the radio. I had a pounding headache and felt too disgusted to talk. Rosie was a lost cause, as far as I was concerned, and was heading into another dark and dangerous situation.

Ultimately, this was just an experience for me, and I would move on from it. Unfortunately, Rosie must have told her boyfriend everything that had happened because that night I was energetically attacked, feeling knives in my back. I continued to have nightmares for at least a week. They were bad in the beginning, but after I smoked out my bedroom with some sage a couple of times, said my prayers, and used double protection day and night, they finally went away.

18

MEDIUMSHIP

In its simplest form, mediumship is the practice of mediating communication between the spirits of the dead and living humans. The life of a medium, or energy worker, is always educational, and it requires a lot of energy to open up to receive spirit energy, or spirit links. Some of these links can be stronger than others, depending on the spirit you're communicating with. If a medium is talking with or otherwise making contact with a client's grandfather in spirit, for example, and the man had not been a big talker when he was alive, his skills will not have improved. I find there are no set rules, however, and things are constantly changing in the spirit world.

Mediumship gained popularity during the nineteenth century, when Ouija boards were used by the upper classes as a source of entertainment. It's also a powerful tool for spiritual healing, providing insights and healing for those who are suffering grief as it connects them to those who have crossed over safely to the spirit world. In my opinion, natural mediums are generally born this way, as it's something that can only be learned by degrees, unlike with psychics, who can be taught to improve their skills with dedication and determination.

As a medium, confirmation of life after death can be an incredible comfort as it offers healing and evidence that our loved ones are safe after their passage into the spirit world. No matter how deep our grief is when we lose someone, it provides great comfort to know there is proof of survival and to learn that life is eternal.

Mediumship is such a huge subject, and has been part of my life's work for so many years. I was first introduced to it through the spiritualist church, standing on the platform, linking into loved ones in spirit, and giving messages to the congregation that always gather eagerly to receive healing from loved ones. Mediums have been amongst us for years, and attempts to communicate with the dead have been documented far back in early human history. Each person who walks this path has their own individual gift to offer the world.

I've found in my own ongoing work as a student of spirit that most clients, no matter what age they are, will come for answers about their loved ones in the afterlife. After they learn that their loved ones have already safely transitioned, they experience a strong sense of closure and feel ready to move on with their lives.

Once you have embraced mediumship as your life's purpose, it's an enormous responsibility because you're helping people through the grieving process, but it's also very rewarding and there are many highs and lows.

Joe

'Sweetheart, I will always love you. I've told you that so many times,' Joe insisted. Joe, the spirit man, was standing beside me as he delivered his messages of love.

On the other side of the table, his wife and daughter sat listening intently to every word I relayed. Crying loudly and holding each other's hands, they wiped at their endless tears of sadness, pain and grief. I paused for a moment, and they indicated for me to go on.

'We talked about what would happen so many times,' the spirit man continued. 'You know I want you to sell the farm, love. No use hanging onto it. It's a man's job, not for women. Go live in town. Cassie wants to go away and study anyway, and that's what I want, too.'

I continued repeating his every word. 'I'll love you forever, you know that,' he said to his wife. 'You're still beautiful. You haven't changed a bit since the day I met you.' Then he laughed. 'I had the best of you, though, and don't you forget that. I was your loving and stubborn cowboy.' Those were his last words; after that, there was silence.

It had been a long session. As soon as I repeated his final sentence, as if on cue a country song came blasting through the walls from the office next door. Before I could say anything, Joe's wife jumped up, laughing hysterically. 'Oh my god,' she said. 'It's a sign from heaven. I can't believe it, he's here. He's really here. That song used to be his favourite. It's Willy Nelson. God bless him.'

Laughing and crying at the same time, she blew her nose and said, 'Oh honey, I miss you so much.'

Regaining her composure, she told me Joe had listened to that song all through his illness with cancer and it gave him hope and comfort. 'It was his song. He played it in the house constantly and in his truck when we went to town. I can't believe it.' She looked at me with gratitude in her eyes.

Her daughter, who had been sitting quietly, said, 'It's true, Mum, he's here. He must've heard our prayers and knew we were coming today. Can he hear me?' she asked me, tears in her eyes. 'I don't believe it, but it's true, he's here. Oh my God, how did he do that?' She looked around the room, crying and whispering to her dad, telling him how much they missed and loved him. She promised to do him proud with her studies.

At that moment, the song ended abruptly, in the middle of the track. There was silence again.

We all looked at each other in awe, not knowing what to say. Then we all started laughing. I thought how clever Joe had been to get such a strong message of love across to his precious loved ones, especially his beloved soulmate. As his energy finally disappeared, I thanked him loudly for the incredible gift of love he had created that day, which had been nothing but a miracle.

Psychics and Mediums

Like all forms of spiritual abilities, you can learn to be a psychic, but you are born a medium. In other words, you are born with that natural ability. It amazes me how some psychics say they are mediums when they're clearly not. They will sometimes say they can't get in contact with a loved one, and if used more than once, this obvious excuse is evidence that they don't have the ability and the client should be passed on to a medium who does.

I have sometimes made contact with a spirit not long after a person has died, when it's been important for that spirit to get a message of love through to the people left behind.

Just recently I received a call from a client who had been to another medium a friend had recommended highly. I had been away, and the client had been unable to see me. The client told me that during the reading her mother, who had always given messages of love and support, said she had moved on and had no interest in talking any longer. She said her daughter needed to work things out for herself. Horrified, my client phoned me in tears, wanting to know if this was true.

In my experience with this client, she and her mother had had a very strong connection throughout their whole lives. As soon as we had spoken, I laughed as I heard my client's mother in spirit talking in my ear, commenting on how beautiful her daughter's unit looked after the recent paint job. Laughing with happiness, my client thanked me, said she was very grateful for the wonderful reading and was glad her mum still knew what was going on.

In my opinion, the woman my client had seen in my absence probably had little or no mediumship skills, and she covered that up by saying the mother did not want to talk to her daughter.

19

SPIRITUAL HELPERS

In your training as a medium you will have many teachers. I have found the best teachers to be your own spirit helpers, or guides. When we are born, we come with our own guide and angel helper. This loving spiritual being is our main guide or gatekeeper to the soul, and stays with us throughout our life until we die. As we develop spiritually, lifting our vibration, we bring in other guides that teach us things. I have six to eight guides in my spirit team that come in and out of my life, and I also have three that are always working with me because of the work I do as a professional medium, teacher and writer.

When I trance channel, my main guide is a gentle Indian spirit chief called White Feather, who protects me. (He was my father in one of my previous Indian lives.) This gentle soul is what I call the gatekeeper, and his duty is to make sure unwanted or malevolent spirits do not come into my energy field, or cause me any harm.

For my spirit shows and media events, I work mainly with a very wise and powerful guide called Romanov, who helps me with my stage shows and my ongoing work with the media. Before this new, very powerful guide came in, I had been suffering from headaches for a while, and I came to understand that this was happening because there was a shift in my vibration.

For my spirit-rescue work, I work with a guide called Margaret, who was a witch in her day; an Indian called Red Hawk, who helps take the lost souls over to the other side; and a Reiki guide called Dr Lee, who helps heal the lost souls.

As for my closed seances, I work with a young spirit boy called Johnny, and other guides will often come in also. I have other guides who help with healing at the end for all the guests, or sitters, who have helped raise the energy for this to happen.

As writing has been a passion of mine my whole life, I wasn't surprised when a talented psychic artist picked up on Leon, a writer guide I work with on my books, documents, scripts and creative work. I never mentioned anything to her, so I was surprised when she picked up on the energy of this rather quirky character. She did a drawing of him, and when I looked at it, I laughed loudly.

Leon looked rather odd, like an avant-garde funster, rather a delicious-looking character who perhaps worked in the theatre back in his day, during the fifties. He was wearing tight pants, a polar-neck jumper and a black beanie, and had a cigarette hanging out of his mouth, which was set in a large mischievous grin; he looked like a naughty little boy.

Leon, I have learnt while working on my projects, is an artist in every sense of the word. When he talks to me in my head when I call his spirit to come closer, he is loud and bombastic to the point of hysterics, and I can imagine him waving his hands around while he talks in spirit. When I asked for more information about him in a meditation one day, he told me he was an artist/actor in his day, loved music, especially jazz, and was here to help me with my spirit shows, writing and psychic information. His advice to me, and everyone, is to sit regularly in meditation, as it will not only help the creative process, but also open doorways to other realities that cannot even be imagined.

Throughout your work and spiritual journey, guides will often come and go, and when you've finished working with them, they will step aside and allow another guide, or guides, with a new vibration to come in and help with the spiritual journey. This helps with the progression of the soul. Many people I've worked with have told me they've been visited by my guides.

A guide, or guardian, is here to assist you with your everyday life and spiritual contract on Earth. When you have finished your time on Earth your loving guide will travel back with you once again to the spirit world. As the bond and love connection will be so strong between the two of you, it could be understood that a past life may have been shared with this enlightened being. A guide is loving and caring, and may be a relative, friend or someone who has passed over to the spirit world and is now living in spirit. Until you pass over to join your guide as a spirit, they will protect you from negative energies, and stay with you throughout your life, protecting your soul.

When you nurture the bond between your guide and yourself, trust and a natural relationship can develop and be of immense strength, which may help you through the more challenging times in your life. You may have many guides throughout your life, and angels that will come and watch over you. As you develop, different guides will come in, work with you, and go again.

There are many stages of trance mediumship, but mine is not a deep trance state, as I like to remember things. If you want to know more about your team spirit guides, you need to sit in a spiritual-development circle, and over time you will become very proficient.

Angels

Angels are here to assist mankind, and want nothing in return. I have had the honour of working with many angels in my work, including the archangels Michael, Raphael, Uriel and Gabriel, who have brought so much light, love, strong intuition and protection. The residual energy they leave behind is truly healing and inspirational. Angels will always assist, but you have to remember to thank them for that help afterwards.

There is a complete hierarchy of angels. They are ranked in nine categories, and also divided into three hierarchies, which include seraphim, cherubim and thrones. Then there are the dominations, virtues and powers to the principalities, archangels and angels.

Through the simple act of prayer, which is a true miracle on Earth and a direct line to the spirit world, your calls for help will be heard. I have seen angels when I work with past-life regression, as they often come in when people have experienced a tragic death in a past life. They are magnificent beings and teach us many things:

- Life is not serious, so we need to laugh more.
- Creativity comes from humour and letting go.
- Life is beautiful, like the colours of nature.
- We need to bring more joy and play into our lives.
- We learn to trust loving angels, and learn to trust and love ourselves.
- Angels make life happier and easier, and let us know that we are never alone.

- An angel is a guardian and messenger from heaven, and can be called upon for help at all times.
- Angels do not control us; they love everyone unconditionally.
- Angels let us know they are here by our side through the sense of smell; they always have a pleasant sweet fragrance, like roses or jasmine.
- Personal angels are integrated with our higher selves, acting as guides and teachers.
- Guardian angels are with us always, just like our main guides from birth to death.

My Guardian Angel

Everyone has a guardian angel in their spirit team that stands next to them from birth to death. Like the gatekeeper, your main guide, your angel, will stay and does not move on. My own guardian angel is called Cassandra. She is a beautiful, kind and gentle healing angel I have worked with for many years in meditation, and in my work. Her divine and beautiful energy is an integral part of the spiritual team I work with. She is a blessing in my life and I am truly grateful.

I always know when my angel is around as I can feel her presence in difficult times, and the happiness and joy she brings me is indescribable. In times of worry, I will see white feathers everywhere, telling me that she is around and I always know, no matter what, that everything will be okay.

On my first meeting with Cassandra in meditation, I was overwhelmed to think she wanted to work with me, as she is so gentle, humble and soft. This is very different from my own personality, which is probably a bit awkward and mad, as I have a very fast brain. Cassandra has told me many times that her main purpose is to help mankind; to help as many people—and animals—as possible. This is my view, too. I want to educate people about the spirit world, teach kindness, and make a difference in the world.

This delightful light being has not only graced me with her presence, but has also taught me, on so many levels, how important it is that we honour and love ourselves as eternal souls, and never feel for one minute less than others around us. When you learn this simple lesson, this is the energy you give out, and people around you will respect you more. It's like the old saying: What you believe, you become.

My guardian angel also talks about taking time out to nurture ourselves. This is something that's not always easy to achieve, especially if we are busy trying to make a living, and many of us are also trying to please those around us. I make it a point, every day of my life, to reserve time in the day just for me, and I make sure I do something enjoyable each day. This can be something simple like walking in nature, buying myself some flowers, or spending time with like-minded people who have the same philosophies as me.

We have many guides throughout our lives to work with, but we always have a few that stay with us and remain our spiritual friends, protectors and teachers for life. When we no longer need to work with certain guides, possibly because we have moved on to other types of work, they will step back. Because we live in a multiverse, our guides will also work with other people so they move on to their own pathway. One of the most powerful moments I have ever had was meeting my own guardian angel in meditation, rather than having to wait until I return to spirit again.

MEDITATION FOR MEETING YOUR GUARDIAN ANGEL

1. Sit in a quiet space and breathe deeply three times, in and out, to help yourself relax. As you begin to relax, start visualising the colours of the chakras: red, orange, yellow, green, blue, indigo and violet.

2. Using your imagination, find yourself in a sacred space, a place in nature that is full of peace, tranquillity and unconditional love, where you can receive healing and nurturing.

3. Now imagine you are surrounded by the most beautiful flowers, all with different colours and sweet scents.

4. As you relax, you will begin to feel the warm sun shining on your skin and the cool breeze blowing through your hair. You will begin to feel one with everything around you. You will begin to feel lighter; the energy of pure, unconditional love is all around you, making you feel energised.

5. As you gently breathe in and out, take the time to focus on meeting your own guardian angel, the guide that is with you from birth until death.

6. When you are ready, call upon your angel and ask them to come closer and present themselves to you. As you do so, let go of any negativity, overthinking and distrust in your higher self. Know now that this is possible.

7. As your angel moves closer, feel the love. Ask if your angel comes from the light. If you don't receive an answer, or the spirit says *no*, tell the spirit to leave and move on. Keep going until you get the answer you want, which is *yes*. This is important, as we can attract mischievous spirits, often from lower vibrations, that like to play games.

8. Once you get a *yes*, allow the loving energy to come closer and stand next to you.

9. When you are ready, ask firmly what your angel looks like. Do they have a form, male or female or androgynous? Perhaps they are just a colour, or a swirl of energy.

10. When you have an image, ask if they have a name, or a message that you need to hear today. Once you have made contact, you will feel the energy, and it will be easier to call on them for any given problem, situation or issue in your life. All you have to do is call them.

11. When you've finished, thank your guardian angel for coming in, and understand that they're now part of your own spiritual team.

12. Now it's time to say goodbye until the next time you want to call upon your guide. Thank them again for their assistance, and feel all your chakras closing down gently as you slowly come back into the room.

20

GIFTS TO WORK WITH IN YOUR MEDIUMSHIP

Mediums can gather information to give to clients during psychic readings through their highly developed intuition, which communicates with them in several ways: clairvoyance (clear seeing), clairaudience (clear hearing), clairsentience (clear knowing), clairolfaction (clear smelling), and clairgustance (clear tasting).

Clairvoyance

Clairvoyance, or 'clear seeing', is the ability to see anything that is not physically present, such as objects, people, animals or places. It brings divine guidance in the form of still pictures or miniature movies that your mind's eye sees inside your head. Often, when I'm talking to a loved one's spirit or doing a psychic reading, spirit will show me small movies in my mind's eye which I will always give as feedback.

IMPROVE YOUR CLAIRVOYANCE SKILLS

1. Find a quiet space where you won't be disturbed. Sit down and begin breathing in and out very slowly. As you do so, release any fears, negative thoughtforms or imaginary blockages about opening up your third eye. Understand that you are safe and this is a gift you've always had. It's your sacred birth right to use this tool to help you in your daily life.

2. Now feel your third-eye centre, which starts in the middle of your forehead and goes down to your nose. Imagine it being like a muscle that needs to be awakened.

3. As you continue breathing with your eyes closed, feel your third eye slowly open and close, open and close. As you continue to do this, feel your third eye opening more and more; feel this energy expanding into the room.

4. Now imagine sending pure golden light through your third eye, clearing it of any negativity, fearful thoughtforms or unresolved issues you may have. It is safe to use your gift.

5. Try chanting. Chanting is speaking or singing words or sounds with one or two pitches called reciting tones. Chanting may range from simple melodies involving sounds to highly complex musical structures that are continually repeated until the person feels that they have had enough. Chants are like prayers, and are used a lot in spiritual practices. Chanting will also help your third eye open as it raises your consciousness, vibration and energy.

6. Practise with a crystal ball, as this will really open up the third eye for better images. For more effective results, call

on the archangels Michael, Raphael, Uriel and Gabriel for assistance, healing and guidance.

7. If you're having problems, ask for help from a spiritual healer, or spiritual hypnotherapist, especially if you feel you're carrying deep-seated issues on the subject.

Clairaudience

Often when I'm working, I'm able to hear the spirit speaker as if I'm on a phone line. I can always tell if it's a woman or a man. I will often make out an accent, and if the person is foreign they will usually relay their message to me in English. Sometimes the connection will be very clear, and at other times not, in which case I'll ask the spirit to speak up. It depends on who the person was, and how open they are in spirit. If they were not a big communicator, they will generally be the same in the spirit world.

The procedure is centred on your awareness. Listen to the many sounds in the stillness around you each day, mentally counting how many you can hear.

INCREASE AND ACTIVATE YOUR CLAIRAUDIENCE SKILLS

1. Start by closing your eyes and listening to sounds in your home, office or study. Amidst nature is a good place to do this, as you will feel more at peace. Next time you walk in nature, stop and listen to everything around you: the earth, the trees, plants, birds, flies, bugs and other insects.

2. When you take the time, you might be surprised at how many different sounds you can hear. Every living thing around you is energy, which, with patience, you detect.

3. Practise listening to the words and sounds of music, and form a feeling. Also pay more attention to the sound of your friends' and family's voices, including children's. This can often give an indication of what is going on in their lives.

4. Clear your ear chakras, or ear energy centres, with white light. These are located on the outside of your ear and are extremely sensitive. Release any doubts or fears you have about this gift by releasing them to the angels or your guides. When having problems, call on your guide or angels for assistance.

Clairsentience

Always trust your feelings, gut instinct and impressions. Your first impression of 'knowing' someone or something is generally correct and important. Your instinctive feeling about a person or situation is almost always correct and will not go away.

IMPROVE YOUR CLAIRSENTIENCE SKILLS

1. Sit in a comfortable position with your feet firmly on the ground and your back straight.

2. Now bring up the golden energy from the earthstar under your feet and take it up to the transpersonal point, which is above your crown chakra.

3. Continue gently breathing in and out, and as you do this, feel yourself opening up your heart chakra and your higher heart.

4. Call the angels and your own loving guides to assist you, and feel the love until you experience a warm tingling inside your body. Ask your angels, loved ones and guides to come closer, and you may feel a gentle hand or energy on your face, back, leg or arm.

5. Be aware of any smells, like perfume, scents or flowers.

6. Let go of any doubts. Understand that your awareness and emotions are divine gifts you were born with. When walking in nature, feel the energy around you that is coming from the trees, the plants, the rocks, the ground.

Clairolfaction

This is the ability to smell spirit. It is also called paranormal smelling, or psychic smelling. The range is wide, from the scent of flowers and perfumes to foul or putrid smells. Though often part of a wider set of unexplained smells, on their own they are sometimes interpreted as indicating a ghostly presence.

A person with this ability doesn't smell the normal smells that most people can detect; they smell energies. These energies are transformed into smell in the nose. You will often smell cigarette smoke, alcohol, aftershave, perfume, urine or food relating to things the spirit did when they were in the living, and the client will recognise these instantly. Sometimes the spirit smell will linger for days, until their message has been relayed or until they're told to leave. I've experienced this many times in my life, and I know that the smells can be very distinctive and strong, and sometimes upsetting.

IMPROVE YOUR CLAIROLFACTION SKILLS

1. Begin by being aware of all the smells around you.

2. Appreciate the different smells associated with a city, a small town and the countryside.

3. Most people have a particular scent, and when you concentrate you can often pick up the smell of their body or the perfume they're wearing. Have you noticed that when people are sick, they carry a strange smell? This is common, especially with cancer or toxins in the body.

4. Each day, write down what you can smell. Don't overdo it. Understand it's safe to switch off this gift like all your other gifts when not needed.

Clairgustance

Clairgustance, or clear tasting, is the ability to receive taste impressions from spirit. I don't know how many times I've tasted cakes, baked meals or treats the spirit people loved to eat or drink in this life. This lets me know how much they miss these things, as I know for a fact that no one eats in the spirit world. One client loved cigars so much that by the end of the session I could taste the smoke in my mouth. When I told the client this, she immediately knew what I meant. She said her husband was always puffing away at the terrible things after every meal. I also have a tendency to burp—which I don't have control of and which can sometimes be uncomfortable—when I taste or feel illness in the body of the spirit person.

21

DIFFERENT TYPES OF MEDIUMSHIP

My main work is that of a mental medium and spirit rescue. I have my own style and my own spirit team, which I rely on heavily, and I never copy anyone. As we live in a multi-dimensional world and are constantly growing, energy is changing all the time.

My best gift is clairaudience, or clear hearing. I'm able to hear the spirit person talking in my ear as though speaking on the phone. I listen carefully, and then all the other senses kick in. It's no surprise, therefore, that these days most of my work involves phone readings. All I need to do is sit back and repeat what the voice I'm hearing in my ear is saying.

Spirit will often work with everything the medium already knows. With my experience as a trained nurse, I'm also able to feel the different organs in the body, and I can describe what it was like for the spirit person to suffer from a particular illness while in the living. I have a grounding in knowledge about many illnesses due to my medical training.

For example, for a spirit that had an enlarged heart in the living before they died, I will be able to discuss the difficulty they had with breathing and the fluid retention they may have suffered with their legs, making it painful and difficult to walk. Knowledge like this gives the client evidence that I have their loved one with them, as they will often be able to confirm what I say.

When I do my stage shows, or work with clients and churches, my guide, Romanov, stands on my left side. He lines up all the spirits in a queue so they don't jump in when I'm working, to help make the connection clearer. Sometimes a few spirits will try to come in at the same time, and when this happens I will ask the guide to separate the spirits and go to them individually.

For example, I might call out the name Bill, referring to a man who died as a result of suicide, and two people will put up their hands. In this case I need more information from the spirits that have come through. When I receive that information, I may say, 'Okay, I have a young Bill, a man in his thirties, and I'm also picking up an older man in his fifties.' Once the two spirits have been separated, I can usually feel which spirit I am with first. This is often helped by a pulling sensation directed at the appropriate person in the audience.

I will go to the first spirit person, give the reading, describe the person, listen to the messages and complete the reading. Then I will move on to the second spirit.

Sometimes I may encounter spirits walking around near the client, or standing next to them; I can often see a clear picture of them in my mind, usually doing something, or a small movie being played.

In my early days as a medium I had all sorts of gifts to choose from to work with in my development. One gift was being able to hear animals' and people's thoughts, which could be unpleasant when I was bombarded with them.

This happened out of the blue when I had my second child. I was walking up the hill from my home and I could hear a voice complaining about fleas. When I looked around, I realised it was coming from the neighbour's dog. When I got to the cafe to meet up with the other mothers, I suddenly found that I could read their thoughts; what they were thinking was not what they were saying. It was an awful experience, so I asked spirit to take it away. It was something I didn't need at the time, with my hormones all over the place.

Trance Mediumship

Trance mediumship is an aspect of mediumship that influences your spiritualty. It's the ability to blend your energies with the spirit control and the medium. It occurs when you subdue your conscious mind, thus slowing down your thinking so the spirits can impose their minds on yours in order to establish their presence. In this state, you can be in touch with and at one with minds that influence, educate, uplift and inspire.

In order to achieve the state of trance, you must withdraw your awareness from the here and now, and move your mind into that aspect of stillness. As you do this, the spirit world will move closer to the medium until there is very little awareness or consciousness with the medium.

When you develop sufficiently to achieve the trance state, it means you have gotten out of your own way of thinking, and blended with the spirit energy.

Trance mediumship involves a special relationship with guides that work with you. This helps build rapport, and can bring a sharper, more specific and accurate flow of information in all areas of healing, mediumship, philosophy and teaching. This is the best way to learn who your own spirit team is that you are working with, as these are the spiritual teachers that will constantly help and educate you along the way.

Channelling Mediumship

This is a beautiful and natural light form of communication between all entities, psychical and physical. I have even channelled nature spirits and I found them very entertaining, especially the little undines, or water spirits, called fairies. My favourites would have to be angels and ascended masters; angels in particular have a very high energy frequency.

Channelling is safe, but I advise you to always close down your chakras after you've finished opening up by imagining them as little lights that are slowly winking out.

As you channel, you're allowing yourself to be an interpreter of the information you're receiving. This is quite an easy process, because once you've found a quiet place all you have to do is close your eyes and the link can be easily made. Once you've done this, the flow of non-verbal information and communication will begin.

The funniest time I can remember was when I ran an intensive workshop with flowers and nature spirits. By the end of the session, everyone was busy channelling fairies and it sounded like a room full of naughty children, their high-pitched voices all talking at the same time.

Once I had closed down the group, we could hear the loud chatter of many birds calling out to each other. Not understanding what was going on, we stepped outside and to our amazement saw ants, insects, butterflies and bugs everywhere. When we looked at the roof of the building, we saw dozens of different types of birds that looked like they were having some type of conference, obviously attracted to the energy of the day.

Everyone laughed. We could hardly believe our eyes. It had been a wonderful experience working with nature's energies.

Transfiguration Mediumship

A transfiguration medium has the ability to communicate, like other mediums, with those in the spirit world. It's about blending vibrations and energy with the spirit in question to forge the connection.

The very first time I saw this done, I was in my early days as a medium. I was in a private sitting with a very talented medium in the spiritualist church who was teaching us trance mediumship. As she went under in a trance state, I couldn't believe my eyes when I saw another person's face instead of hers. As she spoke to the person in the group, we all gasped, as her face had become that of a man's. In fact, it was the deceased father of one of the sitters.

Once the message had been delivered, her face turned back to normal again and she slowly came back into the room. I looked around, and every one of us had tears in our eyes. It had been a very moving, sad and emotional experience.

When I run my own seance groups, often the sitters will say they are able, as we always have a red light on, to see different faces each time I bring through a spirit person. When the guide comes through, the sitters have often said that they have seen the face as well.

Physical Mediumship

Most physical mediumship is presented in a darkened or dimly lit room. I often use a red light, which encourages spirit activity in the room. The spirits make use of a traditional array of tools and appurtenances, including spirit trumpets, spirit cabinets and levitation tables.

Physical mediumship can also produce materialisation of apports, which is the paranormal transference of an article from one place to another, or the appearance of an article from an unknown source that is often associated with spiritualistic seances. Materialised objects can be flowers, jewellery, crystals, stones and shells.

The production of the apports was and still is one of the most prominent and effective aspects of seances. Their behaviour varies from flying through the air, to hitting the sitters in the face, to landing on the table or in people's laps. Favourites are to scatter perfume over the audience, which is quite incredible, or to produce cool air.

The only apport I managed to get was a large stone, which dropped out of the ether one night in my seance room. The rock, or apport, which came from the room next door, was on the windowsill and fell into one of the sitter's laps.

Not a lot of people understand what goes on in a seance, often due to fear, or judgement from so-called experts or sceptics who find great pleasure in ridicule, or are out to prove that seances are fraudulent because these people don't have the intelligence to think outside their tiny square.

Table Tipping

Table tipping is a great way to open up to the spirit world for people just starting out, and it's also a lot of fun. It's also known as table turning or table tilting. It's a paranormal, or supernatural, activity in which participants communicate with spirits by asking them to move a table as evidence of their presence. The group will gather around the table, place their hands on it and then attempt to invoke spirits by calling them. The medium will generally get their guides to step in and assist while the group is running, and you don't have to sit in the dark or use a red light.

Table tipping is very common among spiritualist groups, and has been a part of seances and other practices for centuries. Protection is always used from beginning to end.

22

CONDUCTING A SEANCE

The first seance I ever went to was run by a trained medium from the local spiritualist church I had attended for many years. In the group, we were told that as sitters we would all have a turn at being the main channel, working with our spirit team in trance. We would normally have sat in a darkened room in a large cabinet structure, but in this case we sat on chairs away from the others. The group directed energy to the medium, whose turn it was to go into trance, create the phenomenon, and bring through the messages that would come from the guide or spirit people.

As the medium went under, it was easy to see the spirit overshadow her, a process called transfiguration. The woman was a very good teacher, and we were all encouraged to have a go. At first I was fearful, because I've been terrified of the dark since my experiences as a young child. As spirit has it, everything is preordained in our lives since before we're born, because of our spiritual contracts. Before long, I was learning much about the spirit world I did not know.

Being only a five-minute walk from my home to the church was too easy ... for my cats. I arrived one day to see one of my cats sitting comfortably on a chair at the side of the circle, waiting patiently for me to arrive. All my cats had sat in on my trance and meditation classes for years, or hung around outside the doors to my small office where I held classes, so, although amusing, it was no real surprise to see him there, and it did give me great comfort. When I called his name, he tried to ignore me, and this made the other sitters and mediums laugh. It definitely broke the ice.

After about a year, feeling confident with the training, my guide suggested that I set up my own group with people who were more like myself.

Running My Own Home Circle

After receiving the message, I decided to run my own seance group with a more like-minded group of gentle souls and sitters. Spirit was guiding me to lead my own group and be the person to go under into trance, to receive all the messages. It also didn't suit me being a sitter, as I was sick of spirits sticking their fingers in my back or hitting me on the head. It also got rid of my fear of the dark, as I was safe and protected by my guide when I went under.

My chosen sitters were kind souls on my own vibration and were more than happy to support me, as well as have a fantastic experience. They were all students I had met in my other groups over the years.

Around the same time, I visited a lot of different seance groups to gain experience. Some of the psychical mediums I saw were really good, with a great deal of experience and excellent training. One remarkable man, a German medium, was very encouraging. He told me, laughing, that I had a lot of English spirits, or guides, working with me in my spirit team. From that day on, I never looked back. His kind message gave me the encouragement I needed to continue.

I knew that when you're sitting once a week, you become very sensitive, so I ran my group once a fortnight. Wanting to know as much information as I could, I also researched an English psychical medium, an expert in his field, who had experienced many years of seance phenomena and dramatic communications from famous and ordinary people. I was especially interested in his work with the Scole experimental group he ran, and the work he did with the spirit of Winston Churchill.

When I read of the great work this man had accomplished, I saw this as a sign that anything is possible. I was excited to use my group as an experimental closed group as well, with the same sitters who, after many years, still sit with me today. This group took on a life of its own, bringing messages from not only the sitters' relatives who were in the room, but also famous people who chose to drop in from the worlds of music, the arts and sport.

I never asked for anyone to come in; I left it up to the spirit control, a young spirit boy called Johnny.

A Closer Look at Seances

If you have an interest in psychical mediumship such as seances, you'll be shown another world, but first you need to do a bit of research so you have an understanding of what goes on. The first thing is to watch someone, as a sitter, who does this work and has a good reputation in the industry. I recommend that you wear comfortable dark clothes, not light or bright clothing.

If you feel that you have what it takes, when you're in the flow and feel a calling, make the time to look for an established group that offers training in psychical mediumship. Remember that with all types of mediumship you need to have the right spirit team that wants to work with you and progress you through the many levels. Not everyone will have success, no matter how much time they put into the training, and most often it's because of their spirit team.

Again, you need to sit in a group with a trained medium who has a good reputation, is trained in trance work and knows exactly what they're doing. This work is not for the novice. Ideally, they should have years of experience, and also work with a person who acts as a control. The control is a person who runs the group throughout the session, and helps bring the spirits through by introducing them to the group. For example, they might say: 'I'd like to ask the medium if there's anybody who wants to come through tonight.'

The seance room is always darkened. Some mediums will use a cabinet, which can be used like a very small room, or sit in a chair away from the group. There is usually a small table as well, placed between the medium and the sitters. (I like to use a red light to activate the spirit energy. With trance work I use a blue light.) The medium may also choose to have their hands tied, and agree to being searched to make sure they have no tokens to throw into the middle of the room, which is fraudulent.

It's my firm belief that when doing any type of spiritual work, it's important to set up protection before you start, and to get the sitters to close down their energy centres, or chakras, afterwards. This is done by the control. who offers a prayer while opening the group at the beginning of the session and again when closing the group down.

The prayer usually starts like this: 'Great spirit, we ask to work in the light. Let love and light be our guides. We ask to work in the light always, and ask for protection always.'

When the night is over and the medium is ready to come back into the room, the energy is closed down again with a prayer, and any lingering spirits are asked to leave and go into the light.

Seances are not silly games for ignorant people wanting to have a laugh; they are to be treated with respect. It's a beautiful way of connecting to, and receiving heartfelt messages from, loved ones in the spirit world, and to receive healing from the spirit world, as spirit goes to great lengths to make the connection. Everyone needs to be open-minded. They must be aware of sending good energy to the medium, and focused, to help create the energy and links for the medium to build up in the room.

There's no room for any type of mind-altering drugs or alcohol in my groups, and the sitters need to respect this. I never allow in anyone who is a heavy substance abuser as it is my preference for the energy to be clean. I once had a potential sitter ask to sit in with my group, but I said no as I knew she was a daily pot smoker, something I would not tolerate.

As spirit generally controls the outcome of the group energy, anyone who is not compatible with the energies will usually be moved on by the medium's spirit team in very subtle ways, and will not return to the circle. When people leave, they are energetically cut off from the group's oversoul by the medium, making it impossible for them to tune in energetically to what's going on at the next meeting.

No jewellery such as watches, necklaces or bobby pins are allowed, as these can be moved around by the spirits during the seance.

One woman, a sitter, who did not listen to my rules, had a spirit try to rip out one of her earrings. Going by her screams, I'm sure it was very painful.

Be aware and respectful of the rules set by the medium and the control running the group. The seance is held at a designated time, and once the group is open and the process has begun, the doors are closed. Latecomers are not welcome because they would break the energy once the seance has started.

During a seance, we work only with loving higher entities, and loved ones who come with messages of love, information and healing. We don't talk to lower entities in the astral that have not crossed over to the spirit world, and are troublesome and looking for mischief.

Who we sit with is also important, because everyone is blending their energies and working together as one, assisting with the energy for the medium, who is in a trance state. The group is also working with their own spirit guides, as well as the medium's spirit team.

The Seance Begins

Once the sitters are ready, the person who is the control opens with a prayer of protection. From this point on, the control person runs the group, asking who the medium is with, and ensures that no one leaves their seats until the medium, who goes into either a light or deep trance, is back in their body. Then the group is closed down.

There is only one person who goes into a trance state to lead the group, and that is the designated medium. Some people, however, don't like rules. I once had a student who, unbeknown to me, decided to go into trance as well, and started bringing messages through on his own, without my or the group's permission. I had to close down the group immediately, with the help of my main control, who ran the group for me when I went under. Once I was back in my body, we kicked the offending person out and told him never to return as he obviously had no respect for the rules.

After the group has been opened with the prayer, we play uplifting music while all the sitters sing along. Singing songs and playing music lifts the energy in the room, and encourages loved ones and spirits to come and join us. We also have a traditional array of tools and appurtenances, including a spirit trumpet, a small levitation table that spins all night, and other toys that are used by the spirits.

Other types of phenomena can include knocking on walls, being touched by spirits, the appearance of spirit voices, tables spinning and rocking without help, cones being lifted, bells ringing, lights flashing, orbs, and the sensation of cold or hot air. It can also include spirits, including spirit children, walking and running around the room, created by ectoplasm taken from the cells of the medium and sometimes the seance attendees.

There may also be transfigurations of different spirits over the medium. When this happens, it's of course very moving for all the sitters.

With more experienced psychical mediums, you can often see materialised bodies, including heads, hands or feet, and spirit people walking around the room.

I have never used human batteries like some mediums I have sat with. This is when the medium will use other people's energy to go under by getting them all to hold the medium's body so the medium can draw on their energy. I find this distasteful and not necessary for my own work. It should be an enjoyable experience for everyone in the room. There's always a lot of activity, and I like my sitters to be present and enjoy the experience.

Once the energy starts to slow down, the medium will tell the group the session is coming to an end. The control person will then close down with a prayer, and ask for any remaining spirits to leave and not linger. Once this has been done, the group is finished. The lights go on and there is usually a discussion about what went on.

It's important to note that during a seance we're not working with spirits lost or in the astral. In the event that this does happen, the medium will, with the group, do a rescue and send the spirit back into the light, to the spirit world.

After the Seance

Through my seance experiments, I feel that I'm only a novice, and I know there are far more advanced psychical mediums than me. Again, I stress that it takes a lot of patience, and years of regular sittings. It's still a learning experience for me, even though I've been sitting for many years.

I've worked with highly evolved beings from other planets, and I'm gratified to know that I've been able to heal sitters in the room with some of the spirit doctors I've brought through, people who have lived in other centuries. One woman had to have an eye operation, and with the healing energies the eye slowly recovered by itself. After a healing, the spirit doctors always advise the person to use white sheets on their bed, like in a hospital, and to call them in so they can continue working on them while they sleep.

Spirit doctors have also told sitters to call them in whenever their assistance is needed. Many of my sitters have phoned to tell me how things have gone after the session, and they will often report that their illness or disease has improved, and certain parts of their bodies have been healed.

Psychical mediumship is rare. It takes years of dedication, with regular sittings and dedicated, good people. It's something you cannot rush, as this aspect of mediumship is run by the spirit world. If your spirit team doesn't want you to sit, the group will be closed down, or you will have poor results, which will seem like a waste of time.

Closed Seance and Psychical Group

My private sittings are always joyous occasions, like parties, with lots of laughter, singing and entertainment. It always makes me smile when I go under as the medium in these group sessions. I can hear them while in trance, laughing, singing songs and carrying on while I bring in messages from loved ones, spirits and healing energies.

After years of donating money to the children's hospital, one day we were joined by the young spirit boy called Johnny, who, together with my main guide, said he wanted to work with us as well. Other spirit children came and introduced themselves through the medium. Johnny joined our session, and now works together with my guide, Romanov, who always stands in the background. The energy from that day was remarkable, as it seemed to change the whole group dynamics.

At each session, after we have opened up and said our prayer of protection, everyone sings to build up the energy, which acts as a bridge to the spirit world. This helps with the spiritual phenomena, the spinning of our small table, that turns on its own, and the arrival and departure of the many spirit people who come in during the session.

It's quite common to hear sitters say they can 'see' spirit children, either running around the group or, with their little hands, spinning our small table in the middle of the room. Others have said how they have felt the spirit children jumping onto their laps. Sitters will also feel themselves being touched, experience smells in the room, hear spirit people talking and walking around, and weird noises like banging and knocking or rapping on the wall. Often our small table will be spun around as the children run around the room, and on most nights our music will be stopped and started. One girl said she found tiny feet marks on a newly painted floor.

The other extraordinary thing is that quite often some of the sitters will say Johnny the spirit boy has visited them. He will describe what they have in their house, or what they've been up to. He especially likes cars, and often sitters will say they've seen a small spirit boy sitting in the passenger seat of their car.

As well as the spirits of the sitters' loved ones, Johnny gradually began bringing in celebrities who had been popular in their day. The first was John Lennon, and not long after that Paul Walker, the actor, came in as well. When we asked why he had brought in Paul's spirit, Johnny simply said that Paul loved fast cars and enjoyed riding with Johnny to our special nights. I had no idea who Paul was until I started to watch movies that suddenly appeared on the TV: *The Fast and the Furious*, the American franchise that is still popular to this day and which Paul Walker starred in. I am now a big fan.

We're still visited by many celebrities, who seem to want to come in with messages for the sitters about their own lives. Nothing is ever planned and we never know who will visit us. Every Christmas, we set up a little Christmas tree of gratitude to the spirit children that work with us, with five bright balls in honour of these lovely spirit children that make us laugh and help bring in other spirit visitors.

Private Seance

Following is an example of my practice of conducting a private seance. Once we are all comfortable in our regular seats, the room is completely blacked out; there is no light at all, except a red light to enhance spirit activity. The sitters sit in a small circle.

The group is always opened with a protective prayer and blessing. Jimmy is our main sitter, and has been running the group for many years with the same sitters. He keeps a good, protective eye on everything that goes on, gives instructions to the sitters throughout the night, plays the music on and off, and generally runs the whole thing.

When we open up, Jimmy asks the group to call in their loved ones and guides, then asks for a prayer of protection. Once he has done this, he asks the medium to open the group with her guide, who speaks through her. Our main control is our spirit guide Johnny, and he's the guide that will bring the spirit people through.

When the guide stops speaking, Jimmy asks the group to start singing along with the music, which lifts the energy in the room. Everyone can feel the spirit energy in the room slowly building.

We use a small table that sits in the middle of the group, and it's spun around when the energy gradually builds up. This is similar to table tipping. First the sitters will place their fingers on it lightly for a while to give it energy, then it will start to spin on its own, being pushed by the spirit children that join us during the night. Often the table will jump or spin around madly, as if pushed by the spirit energy and spirit children in the room.

When Jimmy feels it's time, he asks if anyone wants to come through me, the medium. I usually sit on a chair away from the group and in a meditative or trance-like state. Jimmy often says that he can see a transfiguration appear on my face of a spirit being, which is when he will call the spirit in question to come through.

Once the spirit guide has finished speaking through me, I'm able to go deeper into a trance state, gradually bringing energy into the room, creating different types of phenomena, all of this happening while everyone sings loudly to the music.

The sitters will soon start to experience things like flashing lights, orbs, spirit faces in the trumpet, which sits on the small table, and the sound of rapping on the walls. They'll also say they can see spirit people walking around the room, and spirit children running around the table, and many will say they can feel themselves being touched.

We're yet to manifest 'tokens' from the spirit world, but look forward to the day when we can, whatever they may be, whether they're crystals, coins, jewellery or other objects. I'm sure that with perseverance the afterlife has more in store.

By now the room will be freezing. The table in the middle will be spinning around and around in the middle of the group, and spirit people will have begun to come in and speak through me.

After a while the main sitter, Jimmy, will turn off the music and ask if anyone wants to come through me and talk. We generally have a few spirits accept our invitation. Once they've spoken, the control asks the medium if there's anyone else who would like to speak, then the music and singing starts again. This process is repeated until there are no more messages to come through.

Towards the end of the night, which always ends at nine pm, the energy will slowly come down, which is when I call for the spirit doctors to come in and offer healing to the group. Once this is completed, another guide will step in, and Johnny will say goodbye and leave with the spirit children. Then the guide will ask for the group to be closed down, and I step out of my body.

The group will then call me back into the room, and we close down with a prayer. We thank the spirit world and ask any remaining spirits to go back to the spirit world. Then we will chat about the night's occurrences, including what we've learned, and have supper before saying goodnight and finally heading home, full of energy.

It takes a lot of dedication to do this work, and the results will not come overnight. It's extremely rewarding, and we've all enjoyed many years of entertainment and gained insightful information from the spirit world.

Over the years, if the wrong people have been sitting in the group, team spirit has quickly removed them and new people have come. These days my group is closed, and I've had the same people coming who have been with me for years.

It's always amusing to see what happens when I do spirit shows in front of large crowds, as there will always be a lot of spirit activity. People will often say they felt someone touch them, or felt a loved one nearby, or saw a chair move by itself. I've also witnessed banging on the walls, lights flickering on and off, and interference with the music or PA system.

In my group, I have a lot of e-musicians like myself, and the music we play is mostly rock, for instance, 'Sweet Child O' Mine' by Guns N' Roses. Some of our spirit guests have been John Lennon, Frank Sinatra, George Harrison, Jimmy Hendrix, Michael Jackson, Janis Joplin, David Bowie, Prince and Michael Hutchinson.

We've also been visited by actors including Elizabeth Taylor, Paul Walker, as mentioned earlier, Joan Rivers, who is still very funny over there, and Doris Day, who loved animals. After Doris Day came in, the spirits of nearly all the sitters' pets came in as if it was a celebration. I've never in all my years experienced so many pets from the spirit world. I've brought through the spirits of at least seventy-six famous icons, without knowing who was going to come through on the night.

We've also been visited by the great Houdini on several occasions. We've been given instructions on paying attention to the cone, watching for lights, and feeling different types of energy for the spirit phenomena. In one of these sessions the cone was lifted off the spinning table and the sitters said they saw a spirit hand.

23

SPIRIT RESCUE

When we die, most of us cross successfully into the spirit world with our loving guide, angel helpers and, in some cases, loved ones who have come for assistance. Often these visiting spirits gather around the hospital beds of people going through the dying process. We are never alone, as loving spirit is always with us, from birth to death.

Once we've safely crossed to commence our karmic cycle, once again back in the spirit world, our guide accompanies us when we meet with loved ones during a life review. This is when we see all that we have accomplished with our spiritual lessons and learning while on Earth, and have moved on to our different soul groups. Souls that have had a traumatic death stay for a while in a holding space for healing.

Unfortunately, it doesn't always go well. Some spirits become lost, or refuse to cross for a number of reasons. Part of my life's work as a spiritual medium to date is releasing earthbound spirits from entrapment in Earth's plane. This is called spirit rescue. It can be done easily over the phone if the client lives interstate or overseas. If the client lives locally and I have time, I will go to the home, building or land area with another energy worker or dowser to meet the client. Once I've located the spirit or spirits in question—usually by burping, which is how I know that I'm picking up on the energy of the spirit—I'll call in my spirit team for assistance. Using protection and opening a portal of light, I will tell the spirit it's dead and ask it to leave. I tell it to look into the light, as its loved ones are waiting for it on the other side.

There are several reasons why lost souls may be earthbound:

- Suffering a fatal accident
- Having committed suicide (although it must be noted that only a small minority of suicides refuse to cross)
- Fear of crossing over because of some illogical reason
- Religious beliefs holding them back from wanting to go
- Obsessive love or greed for the material world and earthly possessions
- Not accepting that they are in fact dead, and trying to continue living as they would if they were still alive
- Remaining on the physical plane in an effort to ensure the safety of particular loved ones
- Having a strong connection to a particular place, person or item that's preventing them from crossing over
- Thinking there is an obligation for it stay, which can be either a message or some other reason
- Being too frightened to leave with its guardian, angel or loved one because of the actual idea that they are no longer living

Earthbound Spirits

Earthbound spirits are literally everywhere, and a small minority can be seen or felt by sensitive souls and mediums with that ability. They are known to congregate not only in homes and offices but also around large groups of people as they need the energy, or prana, to stay here. Some examples of places are hospitals, railway stations, shopping malls, busy airports, schools, universities, colleges, homes where they once lived, and old theatres. They are rarely found in abandoned graveyards or empty houses, unless there may have been a murder there and that is their last memory.

There are two types of lost souls:

- Earthbound spirits: These spirits go back to a familiar place they knew while alive, for instance the home they lived in or some other special place. In most cases, they don't understand or accept that they are actually dead, and because of this they have no desire to pass over at all.
- Wandering spirits: These are also earthbound spirits, but they are lost and like to follow people around. Some of these spirits can come about through accidents or sudden death. I've experienced these types of spirits from not only ordinary people but also younger mediums or psychics that seem to attract these lost souls because of the light in their aura. This light or energy we have as mediums can act as a beacon of warmth to lost souls living in a very grey world. They are easy to remove.

Residual Hauntings

This is an interesting type of supernatural experience because it's not actually a spirit but rather a recording of specific energy. As everything on the planet is made of energy, energy cannot be destroyed. It's believed that in a location where a person or persons have released a large amount of energy, or experienced heightened emotions, the energy embeds itself, which leads to a type of recording of the events. This is very common in historical places. This in turn keeps repeating itself like a loop, creating a ghost-like effect. This is the most common type of haunting that mainstream paranormal researchers will recognise and study.

Interference Energy

Interference energy is like a portal or small tornado vortex, which may be found in homes and other places, creating a spiritual opening to another dimension. If left open, it can work as s portal to unwelcome guests or spirits from the astral world. This energy can be easily dealt with and closed down by visualising and sending white light into the open vortex. The open vortex will be felt by the hands as a subtle, gentle breeze.

This procedure, which I have mentioned often throughout the book, is used to get rid of any unwanted spirits or negative energy that may be lingering.

SMOKING OUT A HOUSE, ROOM OR SPACE

1. Shut all the windows and doors so the house, or space, is closed off. Make sure you turn off the fire alarm, and don't leave children or pets inside.

2. Take a cooking pot with a lid, and put aluminium foil on the bottom, inside the pot.

3. Place sage that has been pulled into pieces on the foil and light it.

4. When you have a fire, put the lid on the pot to smother the flames so you have thick smoke, as you are literally fumigating the property to get rid of unwanted spirits, negative energy and residual energy. A simple stick won't do it.

5. Start from the front door. With the lid off your pot and a mask on, make your way with the smoking pot through every room, going into cupboards, closed-off areas and difficult spaces. Make sure to carry the lid with you, as you will likely get a big fiery blaze. The lid will stop the fire and create the thick smoke.

6. Once you've finished, go outside and wait for about ten minutes.

7. Open all the windows and doors to allow the thick smoke to escape. You might smell like a bonfire, but you'll be amazed at the shift in energy and the clean feel of the space.

Dianna

Dianna was a client who phoned me six months after moving into her new home, which was very old but had been renovated. She complained about a funny smell, obvious from the first day, that seemed to come from nowhere. She was constantly arguing with her husband, and the kids were having problems at school. Her two cats, which had been healthy before they moved, got sick and died.

Dianna put me on speaker, and as she walked from room to room, I remotely scanned the energy of the house. I sensed that she had two earthbound spirits living in her home. When I described them, she said it sounded like the people who had lived there before them. One was in the master bedroom and the other was in the common room, where the family gathered for evening dinners.

Both spirits were confused and had been there for a long time, but I had no problem sending them over. After I cleared the home, I suggested she give the place a good smoking and things would undoubtedly improve.

24

MURDER CASES AND MISSING PERSONS

For a while I did join a group of mediums and psychics who worked for the police, and together we blended our energies to obtain information on many unsolved cases. I soon realised that there are a lot of missing people in the world, and cold cases that have yet to be solved. We were told not to discuss the work, which was confidential, and I have never done so.

There is no doubt that this work is incredibly important and can be rewarding, so if you're mentally tough enough, a bit of a detective, and you wish to help, you will benefit the community.

Unfortunately, working in this area has a weird and almost creepy energy, as there are often dark spirits and negative energies connected with it. As time went by, I decided it was not for me, partly because every time I came home my family complained that it was as though I was being followed by a trail of negative energy.

I came to realise it was not my calling, and there were other avenues that were also important, like mental medium work, healing and spirit rescue, which I felt far more comfortable doing.

That was also a lesson to me to keep my work and busy business out of the family home. When I rented a space elsewhere, it was perfect because of the energy factor, plus the sheer number of clients I began to see.

These days it's not uncommon for me to get a murder victim or a missing person in a reading, and I'm always happy to give all the information I can to assist the family and loved ones wanting answers, as you can imagine what a terrible time people go through when somebody they love goes missing. Also, I'll always give any information I have to other mediums working on these cases if they ask for my assistance, but I always insist they not mention my name or get me involved; families will constantly make contact if they know you're doing the work.

Connie

Connie, an old friend I hadn't seen for a while, rang in tears one day and spoke about her childhood friend, Josh, whom she had known back in England. Josh had disappeared without trace while on holiday in the south of Spain. Eventually he was classified as a missing person and the case was closed.

As soon as Connie finished speaking, I sensed a strong male spirit energy building up next to me. I heard a spirit man say he was Josh, and as I tuned into his voice, I saw him in my mind's eye: he was tall, with bushy brown hair and a beard. He was dressed in a pair of jeans and a large, flowered shirt. Around his neck was a gold chain and he had a diamond in his right ear. I was confused, because I sensed that he wasn't sad at all, but very cheery.

When I described what I was seeing, feeling and hearing, Connie started crying. I had confirmed that her feelings had been right, and her friend was dead.

The communication from the spirit man was very clear. He had crossed safely to the spirit world and was not confused or earthbound. I listened intently, relaying everything to Connie, word for word. I thought Josh must have been very funny when he was alive; he didn't stop joking and kept referring to Connie as 'thunder thighs'. She took this private joke as a sign that it really was him.

As the reading progressed, Josh showed me what looked like a deserted, windy road in a rough mountainous area. It was early evening and the sky was darkening. He said he had been hitchhiking when two men in a white van stopped. He thought they were offering him a lift, but instead they robbed him of all his money. Before they had time to tie him up, he ran into the thick bush and hid, and eventually the two men drove off.

Lost and confused, he remembered it being cold as he stumbled blindly deeper into the bushy and rocky terrain. He must have become disorientated, because the next thing he described was losing his footing on the rocks in the darkness and falling off a cliff. He couldn't remember much of his death, other than falling and then complete blackness.

Then he said that a blinding white light, like a gigantic tractor beam, had encompassed him, pulling him slowly upwards. He looked down and saw his broken body lying motionless at the bottom of a steep ravine. He could hear water below him.

Then he felt incredible love and his beloved grandfather, who had died many years before, appeared beside him, holding his hand and comforting him.

After I relayed these messages to Connie, who was crying softly, I reassured her lovingly that her friend would not have felt pain or suffered. With traumatic, tragic, cruel and unnecessary deaths involving suicide, murder or accident, the spirit will always leave the body before the impact of death, meaning the person does not suffer trauma or pain of any kind.

Josh also said that as well as his grandfather, many other people he knew appeared as spirits on the other side, so he wasn't lonely. He said it was wonderful to catch up with his old mate Terry, who had died years earlier in a motorbike accident when he was hit by a truck.

When I asked Josh exactly where his body was, he refused to say, insisting that it didn't matter. I knew from my experience in working on cases involving missing persons and murders that it was not uncommon for spirit people to refuse to give details of where their bodies were located.

25

HEALING CURES FOR MEDIUMSHIP

Everybody goes through grief in their own way. Never isolate yourself, and always seek support when dealing with such an emotional time. Know you are not alone and that it's always a good thing to talk with friends and family.

If you're grieving, talking to a trained professional will always be helpful. Find a therapist who works with bereavement and spiritual healing, and when you're ready, consult a good medium. Take good care of yourself, because you are loved and needed here as well. It's also important to understand the stages of grief. Sometimes it's really good to have a pet, as love and comfort come in so many forms.

Try talking to your loved one's photograph. It's amazing how well that can work. Don't worry about whether or not they will hear you; they will. I've even had spirit people tell me not to keep the old photographs of themselves, just the younger ones. Personalities don't change just because someone has died.

Divine Prayer

One of the simplest, easiest and greatest gifts we have is the gift of divine prayer, which is a direct link to the spirit world, the angelic kingdom and our loved ones in the spirit world. You will always find assistance, no matter what you think. Imagine prayer as being like a direct call to the spirit world. Not only will you receive guidance, healing and positive energy when you pray, but you can also send love to your loved ones in the spirit world, which will be greatly appreciated.

This is a prayer I use with all my work when opening up:

'I am the Christ consciousness within,
I am a clear and perfect channel of love and light,
Let love and light be my guide.
Thank you.'

And I use this prayer when closing:

'Thank you spirit for your divine presence with us today.
As we depart from this special time and space,
We ask you to clear the space from any darkness, or earth-bound souls
And ask them to return to where they came from.
We also ask for a blessing always in our daily lives.
Thank you.'

If you are a wise woman or man, a healer, pagan, wizard or white witch, you will have your own opening and closing prayers when working with different rituals.

Call on the Angels

An angel is a universal being of light whose soul and single purpose is to help us here on Earth. Angels act as messengers, protectors and guardians of hope, and can come in the form of visions, intuition, knowing and dreams. They love us dearly and are always around to comfort us. I've always believed in angels, and have asked them for assistance with healings for as long as I can remember. But they will often test us, as well.

One hot summer day, I was at the local train station waiting for a train into the city. All I could think about was having a cold drink and getting on the train as fast as I could. I tried to squeeze under the little bit of shade there was. There was no one at the station, which seemed rather odd. As I stood there alone, what looked like a homeless man approached and asked me for money so he could buy a drink. The man was dirty and haggard, and smelled of rotten food. When he spoke, I could see his brown teeth.

I reached into my pocket and gave him all my change, which amounted to about twenty dollars. As soon as I handed the money to him, he smiled the most beautiful smile. I turned away in embarrassment, thinking maybe it wasn't enough. I was just about to remember my manners and thank him as well, when he disappeared. The platform was empty. There was no explanation for how someone could disappear as quickly as that.

Later, in meditation, I was told the man had been an angel and that I was being 'tested', whatever that meant. I didn't know then and I don't know now. All I do know is that angels can take human form. Many people think of angels as having long white gowns and big wings, like you see in the churches, while others see them as pure energy and light.

Call on the Ascended Masters

An ascended master, deity or cosmic being is simply pure loving energy and frequencies made of light. They are high frequencies, or high energies, which can be used through meditation. They are easy to access, and helpful when going through negative, sad and troubling times. These beings, pure energy of light, are here to assist us through the trials and tribulations of our spiritual lessons in this lifetime.

Some of these beings once lived on the planet, and through their own endeavours and hard work have paid all their karma, left the cycle of rebirth and attained mastery over themselves. They are beings of light, and not physical bodies. In meditation, these great, loving and magnificent higher beings always bring more light onto the planet, and come with great healing. They are especially good to connect to in difficult times as they are always here to lovingly help with their powerful magic, energy, messages and spiritual insights.

It has been a great experience and humbling honour for me to work with these light beings, and a pleasure to now share this information with you. When you start to call in the higher energies—ascended higher masters, angels and goddesses—you will notice the change in your life straightaway. Your mindset will change, you will be inspired, and your intuitive powers will grow on a daily basis. These heavenly light beings not only have great wisdom and power, and can help you tune into your own psychic abilities, but they are also available when you pray or call on them. Throughout the world, they have always worked behind the scenes and have long been shrouded in mystery.

Quan Yin

Quan Yin is one of the most beloved and popular Eastern divinities and is known as a *bodhisattva*, an enlightened one. Her energy is compared to what a mother feels for her child, as it is so caring, kind, loving and protective. She helps everyone and is known as the goddess of mercy, compassion and protection; her name means 'she who hears prayers'. Quan Yin is often called the 'Mother Mary of the East' because she represents feminine divinity and goddess energy in the Buddhist religion, in the same way that Mary radiates sweet, loving femininity within Christianity.

It is said that she answers every prayer sent her way, no matter who or where it has come from; she does not discriminate. Her energy helps us fully open up to our spiritual gifts, and attain spiritual knowledge and enlightenment. The mere uttering of her name is said to afford guaranteed protection from harm.

Quan Yin teaches us to practise a life of harmlessness, using great care to ease suffering in the world and not add to it in any way. She's known to help us with compassion, clairvoyance, kindness, gentleness, sweetness, love, mercy, singing and spiritual enlightenment.

Years ago, I ran a meditation group for students. Each fortnight, I would introduce a new master energy for everyone to experience, and I have to say that I have never felt so much gentleness and peace as the night I worked with Quan Yin's energy. As she transfigured and overshadowed me, so very gently, I could feel a rush of love and compassion wash over me, and down to my heart chakra.

After I closed down the group energy and instructed everyone to close down their chakras and come back into the room, all the sitters said it had been the same for them as well. They all shared their beautiful experience with the others, and there was not one person in the circle who was not affected that night. During the meditation, they could all feel gentle waves of soft and warm energy washing over them, constantly, as if washing away all the troubles they had been holding onto.

As we went around the circle, some said they could also detect the strong smell of jasmine lingering in the air, which reminded them of spring. Others were crying, saying they felt they had received healing; they were able to let go of their problems and pain, and felt so much lighter.

Quan Yin, once you discover her powerful energy, is a good friend to have in your spiritual circle of friendships. Her energy can be called on in any crisis in your life. Her beloved energy works very fast and she helps millions of people of all faiths. Peace comes in many forms and will sweep away all pains.

QUAN YIN MEDITATION

1. Sit quietly in a space where you will not be disturbed, and light a gold candle. Now place some rose-quartz crystals on the altar, for love. Add a piece of celestite to connect to the divine energy and cosmic supernatural forces for spiritual strength and inner peace, and a few white feathers for spiritual insights and messages. You could also place a piece of white selenite next to Quan Yin for cleansing and clearing; this will be good for you, and also your home and space. (I love the smells of lavender, clary sage or sandalwood when working with this energy.)

2. As you take three deep breaths, go quietly into your inner stillness. Now, say out loud and clearly: 'I now call on you, Quan Yin, in all your beauty and loving wisdom. I ask for your assistance, guidance and divine loving healing. I call on you today to bring peace and harmony into my life. I humbly surrender all my problems and pain now. I kindly ask for assistance to move on and release all grievances I have against people who may have not been kind. I ask for an intervention and a miracle to help with this problem. I ask, with great gratitude, for a healing and good outcome. May spirit bless you, the planet and everyone in my life. Thank you, and may great spirit always bless you.'

3. When you've finished, close down all your chakras and energy. Expect a miracle, healing or insight within a short time of the meditation.

26

SPIRIT SIGNS

Spirit signs will always touch your heart and soul with hope, healing and love. This is spirit's way of letting you know there is life after death, and your departed loved ones are simply in another dimension, which is just a hand's length away. No matter what you believe, I ask you to be open for signs or spirit messages from your loved ones, as they are always there. These signs or messages of love from loved ones in the spirit world can come in many different forms, including:

- Shooting stars: Seeing a shooting star is often a sign that everything is going to be okay. Don't forget to make a wish, too, as these are often part of your dreams of where you see yourself in the world.
- Feathers: They can be all colours and shades, and can appear randomly right in front of you. Whenever I'm in trouble or going through worrying times, I'll always receive a whole collection of feathers. When I tune in to the energy of a feather, it generally gives me a message that is very healing, telling me that everything will be okay and I have nothing to worry about. It also means someone who loves me in spirit is close to me.

- Coins: Like feathers, coins can appear out of nowhere. You can find them in your clothes, on the ground, or sometimes in your bed. Personally, this always reminds me of my grandfather, who is always around me in spirit in troubling times.
- Perfumes, signature scents: I have often heard clients say they can smell their mother's perfume around them, or their father's aftershave.
- Music: How many times have you heard a song out of the blue that reminds you of a loved one, or a piece of music that was a favourite of your loved one? There are no coincidences in this world. As the spirit world is naturally a higher vibration than we are in the physical world, spirit often finds it easier to connect to the vibration of music.
- Street names: You may be thinking of someone, and then suddenly see their name on a street post, billboard or building, or in a book, or hear their name spoken on TV.
- Butterflies, birds and dragonflies: It's amazing how nature will often provide a way for spirit to get a message of love across.
- Cigarette smoke: I don't know how many times I've smelt cigarette smoke when the loved one was a smoker. Smoke often lingers in the air when the loved one is around. I'm sure that if some of the loved ones I've talked to could have smoked in spirit, they would have. It's a very hard habit to get rid of.
- Dreams: Our dreams, which can be vivid, come from the subconscious mind and vary in length, content and the simple information they impart. Dreaming can be an incredible experience, to say the least. Dreaming is a good way for our loved ones to come through and leave messages of love, as it is an easy way for them to communicate. Dreams can be emotional and quite

profound, and even feel surreal, as though the loved one is right there. Dreams can also vary in emotion, ranging from happy to sad, and leave behind strong residual energy.

- Rainbows: These are a common symbol for love, and many say that rainbows always make them remember their loved ones, and let them know they are sending a message from the other side.
- Clouds: How many times have you seen subtle messages in the clouds? Whether it's faces or something else, it's amazing what you can see when you're open to this type of phenomenon. Subtle messages from spirit can come to you in so many ways.
- Spirit orbs: This is a common phenomenon that is easier to see with a camera than the naked eye. If you see orbs, they are likely to be as delighted as you are. They can look quite extraordinary. Orbs are actually spirit lifeforms that travel around, and are believed to be the human soul or life force of those who once inhabited a physical body here on Earth. Depending on the size of the orb, if you look closely, you may be able to see a tiny face inside.
- Ghost orbs: These are bigger, thicker and denser in appearance than spirit orbs, and are generally dark. However, although they are bigger and thicker, they can be harder to see and are not as common as the spirit, or nature, orbs that seem to appear naturally. Although harmless, ghost orbs can be a disruptive and negative energy to have around, as they can make life difficult by drawing in negative energy to your space. Orbs can be easily smoked out with good-quality sage.
- Spirit orbs: These are usually lighter than ghost orbs, although they can vary in shape and size. Some appear as tiny pinpricks, while others can be as large as an

apple or orange. I see these orbs as tiny shining lights that glisten like stars. They are beautiful to look at, and some people call them angels.

- Spirit orbs are our loved ones or friends from the other side, or healing guides or spirit doctors. Their message is always the same: to let their loved ones know they are safe and have survived death.
- Nature orbs: These appear as tiny lights that we see in nature, and are more common around water. They vary in shape and size, like spirit orbs. They seem to accumulate in large groups, and you will usually see a whole lot of these transparent, shining orbs bobbing up and down all over the place in nature, and especially above water. These elemental spirits are incredibly healing.
- There are four types of nature orbs: salamanders, sylphs, earth spirits and undines. Each is different, but all coexist in harmony, and are active in our great forests or anywhere on Earth where there is an abundance of grass, flowers, trees, water and wildlife. I've seen many undines, or water fairies, in the form of little lights or opaque orbs, around rivers, lakes, waterfalls or rocky ponds.
- Children and pets: Often kids can be of service as 'little messages' from spirit. As they are so open energetically, our loved ones can easily connect with them. I have heard many stories of children often talking about loved ones in spirit. Pets are the same and can often sense our loved ones in spirit.
- Blown light bulbs: It's easy for spirits to manipulate electricity and cross wiring, as they are themselves forms of energy, albeit vibrating at a higher frequency. Often lights will flicker in a home when they are around, just to let you know they are there to say hello to.

- Clocks: Clocks will often stop when spirit comes to visit. This is spirit's way of letting you know they are visiting.
- Soft and gentle touches: I have had many clients tell me how they felt themselves being touched gently on the face or shoulder when going through difficult times.
- Spiritual apports: According to parapsychologists and spiritualists, an apport is the paranormal transference of an article from one place to another, or an appearance of an article from an unknown source that is often associated with spiritualistic seances. Materialised objects can include flowers, men's and women's jewellery, crystals, stones, shells, and even live animals. Apports of flowers have been traced to a nearby garden. The production of the apports was and is still one of the most prominent and effective aspects of seances. They can vary from flying through the air, to hitting sitters in their face, to landing on the table, or in people's laps.
- A sign from your loved one that only you understand: When I think of my aunty, it's amazing how I will see and hear things she loved when she was in the living, like red lipstick, loud laughter, or simple words overheard in other people's conversations. Sometimes you will see little flickering lights in your peripheral vision. This is generally a loved one or angelic energy letting you know they are around and with you.
- Apparition: These can be unexpected and extraordinary. They can take the form of a loved one, a ghost or an animal, and can have many forms, especially in nature, similar to the spirit faces you may sometimes see that appear out of nowhere on a tree, rock or in the water. Sometimes these spirit faces that appear are messages, warnings or greetings.

I once encountered an apparition while travelling overseas, while in a dangerous situation. We were in a small boat, and large waves started coming over the sides. The boat was also overloaded with people, which would not have helped. The apparition came in the form of an angel that stood in front of me, giving a warning and shaking his head.

I took notice, and demanded that the driver turn the boat around, telling him the seas were too big. Fortunately for me and the others onboard, he listened, but we later heard that other boats were not so lucky. Some religious people have claimed to see holy apparitions as well; as mediums, we are always hearing stories of such things.

27

VISION WALK

Often in life we need as much help as we can get when going through difficult times. A vision walk is a good technique to use when looking for signs that your loved ones are around you in spirit and supporting you, telling you they're near, finding resolutions to complicated problems you might be going through, helping the creative energy flow for ideas and inspiration, offering spiritual insights and so much more. A vision walk is basically a stroll through nature, where you get to connect to your higher self, or inner knowing, to find answers you may need at this point in your life.

I use this exercise a lot as it helps me channel, and whenever I'm missing a loved one I'm forever receiving signs, which gives me so much comfort. Often I can almost feel my loved ones in spirit by my side, along with my angel helpers and guide. I will also get answers for confusing problems I may be having in my life.

CREATING A VISION WALK

1. Before starting on your walk, make sure you're wearing comfortable clothes and a hat, and take some water. Switch off your phone and any other electrical gadgets so you're not disturbed. If walking with a friend, there should be no talking as the mind needs to be open and the senses aware.

2. Before you begin, think of something you need an answer for.

3. Now begin walking. Along the way you may see many signs from spirit: feathers, smells, messages in the clouds, street names, birds, butterflies, numbers, number plates of cars, flowers, songs, food, trees, water, waves, boats, to name a few. Everything you need to see will present itself to you when you surrender to what spirit is showing you.

4. When you've finished your walk, sit down and think about what you've discovered. If you're with someone, it's a time for discussion. You can also write everything down in a journal.

5. Let the past go, and know that this is an opportunity for a new day, a new way of thinking. You are always safe and protected, and exactly where you are meant to be now for your spiritual lessons and contracts. Each time you do this exercise, it will help you along the many steps of your journey in life.

Jessica

I once took a friend, Jessica, on a stay-in-silence vision walk. She was going through a difficult time with her relationship, encountering lots of roadblocks, and she was desperate to find a way of not having to worry all the time, especially for the sake of the children involved.

When I suggested we do this walk, she happily agreed, and ended up getting right into it as she had so many decisions to make, plus she had the children to think of.

When we returned to my home after our long walk, Jessica told me about all the signs she had experienced along the way. Among the things she saw was fruit spilled on the ground, which reminded her of wasting money on takeaways and her diet, and she saw white butterflies, which she felt gave her faith. She also mentioned seeing a couple who looked happy and were very playful. This, she said, reminded her that it was time to move on and find the right person; she accepted that she had spent too many years with the wrong one.

The other thing Jessica mentioned was seeing a hearse drive past on its way to a funeral. Laughing loudly, she said this was a sign that one part of her life was ending, but new things would come. She knew it was time to start thinking of the future and rebuilding her life.

28

TRAVEL IS GOOD FOR THE SENSES

As a child, I used to dream of a faraway land of ice and snow, with incredible mountains, high peaks and large waterways, which I realised later were fjords. At this time in my life, I had no idea what this meant because I'd never seen a landscape like it before, and had never experienced snow.

These dreams made me feel uneasy for days afterwards because they always came with a sense of unexplainable sadness and great longing. I don't know how many times I woke up full of sadness in the morning, with a wet pillow after these dreams and visions. My feelings were so raw and real.

After my studies as a teenager, I decided to travel. Travelling was exciting as it opened up all my senses. The different smells, tastes, impressions and feelings whenever a train pulled into a station always excited me. I was never scared, as I believed in spirit and angels, and I knew intuitively that I would always be looked after and protected. If anything did come up and I got a special feeling in my gut, along with negative energy or bad vibes, it was a psychic warning from spirit telling me to protect myself straightaway. Instead of walking into trouble, I would go around it, especially when travelling to remote, isolated and dangerous places in the company of people I didn't know.

Just when I was thinking it was time to stop travelling and look for work, I had a chance meeting on a train with two lovely sisters from Norway who were on a camping trip during their summer holidays. From the moment we met there was a special bond, a connection; the three of us got on so well it was as though we'd known each other our whole lives.

We arrived on the beautiful coast of Croatia and pitched our tents. We spent the rest of that month swimming in the sea, dancing to music every night, and laughing hysterically over stupid things.

The only annoyance was the attention of amorous young men who followed us constantly, in droves, everywhere we went, trying desperately to seduce us with words of love. As soon as the buses pulled in to the stations, these men would be waiting like hungry predators, ready to pounce, smoking cigarettes, drinking beers, dressed to the nines in tight pants and shiny shirts, with their strong aftershave lingering in the air. Luckily for us, one of the sisters embarked on a holiday romance on our first night. He was our knight in shining armour. A tall, strong man with huge muscles, he became our bodyguard, an excellent deterrent against the frisky and amorous young men.

The next few weeks were wonderful and a lot of fun. When the holiday was over, we said our goodbyes to the people we had met and I travelled with the two sisters to Norway, where I hoped I would find work.

As soon as I took my first steps in Norway, with my huge pack on my back, I had a strong and sudden feeling of déjà vu. I felt dizzy. I had the overwhelming feeling that I'd been there before, but a long time ago. I looked around. Everything seemed familiar to me and I felt that I belonged there. It was totally confusing. I was in a place I had never been before.

Closing my eyes, I took a moment and breathed deeply to find clarity, and nearly jumped in shock when I saw flashes of the strange dreams of ice and snow that I had experienced as a child so long ago. I felt overwhelmed with emotion. Perhaps I had been there in another lifetime, but this was now, and the reality was that everything was upside down, as if my hands were on the ground and my legs were in the air.

My senses were on high alert. As I opened myself up to the energy around me, I sensed the varied smells, listened quietly to the different sounds, and stared at the people walking past, as though I might recognise somebody. The whole landscape and energy of the place resonated with me, deep inside my soul, and it was a good feeling. Breathing deeply, I felt my heart pounding in my chest, as though it would explode and, in that moment, I could only wonder what was going to happen next.

When the three of us arrived at the large family property, we were greeted by the girls' mother, Elsa. She welcomed me with a beautiful smile, a twinkle in her eye and open arms. Elsa, I soon discovered, was a kindred soul, someone who possessed an overwhelming spiritual energy. She was an extraordinarily compassionate and loving soul, a warm and kind woman who healed people with her special powers—the radiant golden energy she channelled through her hands. I felt it was a blessing that I had met her, as she was certainly someone to admire. She was a very special soul, and I felt humbled to know her.

Elsa told me her clients were people from the neighbouring towns and villages, and they often travelled long distances to see her, to benefit from her natural herbs, special remedies, medical balms and healing. There were always strangers waiting to see her, and she was constantly busy. She was a very good healer, and much valued in the community.

I came to understand that Elsa had been given her gift to help others when she was young, a gift that was passed down in the family when the appropriate person reached a certain age.

Every time I walked into her healing room, I could sense the warm residual energy, like a psychic imprint that lingered brightly. Whenever I lay on her table, I always felt currents of light energy pulsating from her hot hands, spreading warmly throughout my body and making it tingle.

Elsa never liked to talk too much about her work. She believed there were ignorant people around who would have liked nothing more than to judge her harshly and label her a witch through fear, judgement and petty jealousy. She told me she was mindful of who she saw, and only worked through word of mouth, never advertising her work.

This is a familiar story that has been repeated around the world throughout the centuries during dark and sad times in our history, when women healers who worked as midwives and herbalists, and with the arts, were burnt at the stake, or persecuted by the church as witches. The distrust persists today: anyone who is different can be perceived as odd, and isolated from the community, talked about and scorned. The frugality of the human spirit can be very cruel.

Elsa had the most amazing golden aura, or glow, around her head, and beautiful kind eyes full of light that would sometimes shine back at me. Other times, she would look right through me, something that made me feel nervous at first, because I felt like she was reading me out of curiosity. No matter how hard I tried to block her stare, or look away, it was impossible, as her piercing, penetrating glaze seemed to scan my energy, trying to work out what was inside my head.

Elsa's husband, Bjorn, was the complete opposite of her. He was a very ordinary fellow who never said very much and liked to stay in the background. I think he preferred it that way, accepting that it was the Viking women who ruled the home. He worked most of the time, tinkering in his shed when he was home. A big man with a big belly, in the evening he would sit contently next to the fire and read his newspapers.

On the weekends, Elsa fussed over Bjorn, seducing him with her amazing culinary skills; I never once saw him refuse a meal. It made me giggle to see him lick his mouth greedily after every meal. Elsa prepared great banquets for him, with many different types of meats, sauces and vegetables, followed by stewed fruits, sugared jams, waffles, creamy cakes and warm chocolate puddings. After his meal Bjorn would go back to his favourite chair and sleep for a couple of hours.

In the summer months, I spent time with Elsa collecting wild berries and herbs from the surrounding woods. She would pulp the herbs for her balms, and freeze the berries for later use as fresh jams and sweets. She also collected wild, woody mushrooms that grew not far from their home. In Elsa's small garden, I'm sure she must have given some of her vegetables the leftover healing from her hands because her tomatoes and vegetables were always big, juicy and healthy.

I learnt how to cross-country ski on large planks, and helped to collect groceries from the local shop when we were snowed in during winter. Quite often we skied past wild reindeer that lived in the surrounding mountains. I was terrified at first, but only had one bad experience when I was chased by a large bull with enormous antlers.

Elsa looked at me one day in her knowing way and said that I was also 'special'. She must have picked up that I was psychic and read my energy through the colours in my auric field, which is easy to do when you're an energy worker. Those who work with high healing guides and the angelic realm always have shades of purple and flashes of green, gold and silver at the top of their head. I wasn't surprised that she knew I was a natural medium, and I admitted to her that I had studied and trained in a spiritualist church for three years.

29

PAST LIVES

Past-life regression is just one of the many tools that awaken memories of past lives or incarnations that are buried deep within the soul, which we carry from lifetime to lifetime. It teaches us many things, and can help clear any phobias we may have, and also help us identify patterns or barriers that we exhibit, for instance, in our love lives.

The theory is that we have all lived past lives and we will all continue to live future lives. What we do in this lifetime will influence our lives to come as we evolve karmically towards our own immortality.

During a past-life regression, the subject answers a series of questions while hypnotised, questions designed to help reveal past-life identities and associated events. This technique, using hypnosis, explores deep memories within the souls of past lives or incarnations. We often learn that through reincarnation we have played certain roles or lived in certain places before, and are attracted to the same archetype role or country in our current life. Past-life regression also teaches us about the different soul groups in the spirit world.

When I returned to Australia after my travels, which included living in Norway for many years, I went to a lecture on past-life regression therapy and learned that we carry memories deep within our subconscious minds from all our past lives. I could not get over my experiences, or the connections, or the fact that I was speaking fluent Norwegian within six weeks.

When I had my past-life regression session, I was taken to a past life in Norway, where I had lived the life of a huge male Viking called Tron, who had battle scars and deep wounds all over his massive body. While I felt myself within his body in that traumatic lifetime, I could sense how lost, sad and lonely he was, due to a lifetime of constant battles and living a futile life. The therapist was very good, and it didn't take long for me to understand the blockages from Tron's life and clear them. I had never in my life experienced anything like it.

30

PRECOGNITIVE DREAMS

Precognitive dreams are common and are a natural type of phenomenon showing us the past, present and future. Many people I have met, including clients from all walks of life, have experienced them. You don't have to be psychic to have these dreams, and they can help you avoid potential disasters, or make the right decisions in all aspects of your life, including work, relationships, health, and anything else that comes your way. They can also be warnings of not-so-good things to come, giving you time to prepare your responses.

These dreams are links to the spirit world, which has all the memories from every other lifetime you have ever lived, and are a direct link to the Akashic records, a compendium of all universal events, thoughts, words, emotions and intents in the past, future and present.

If you have problems remembering your dreams, there is an easy way to do this. I always ask my guides to help me.

HOW TO REMEMBER YOUR DREAMS

1. Get a small book to record your dreams in, and place it next to the bed where you can reach it easily.

2. Before you go to sleep, remember to say a little prayer, or mantra, asking spirit to help you take note of all the details. This is very important. If there's a question you want to ask, make sure you remember to ask for an answer, as spirit guides often work through symbols and pictures.

3. Try to make a practice of sleeping with white sheets, as they are extremely good for healing on a spiritual level, and I find that they can help with memory. And, if you think about it, they are always used in hospitals, which are places of healing.

4. Always have a glass of water by the bed, and have a drink before you go to sleep to hydrate your body. I always leave a window open for fresh air, as a stuffy room and smells can interfere with sleep and create jumbled thoughts.

5. When you wake, make a habit of writing down everything you experienced in your dreams before you step onto the floor, or you will forget everything. Take note of colours, as these represent the chakras, just as numbers always represent time.

6. If you do this every night, after a while you'll begin to get a story. The subconscious mind is a powerful tool and explains our conscious realities.

Like anything you do in life, with a lot of practice anything you want to do or accomplish in this field can only improve, helping your psychic abilities increase to a higher level and frequency of consciousness. Happy dreaming.

31

TOXIC SPELLS, MANIPULATION AND ENERGY VAMPIRES

Living overseas in my early twenties was an exciting time for growth in my life as I met so many liked-minded people and had so many life experiences. In one period I was sharing a large house with quite a few people I met in the city, who were all into music. Erik was good friends with everyone in the house and was always there. He didn't officially live with us, but he was a permanent fixture.

Erik was very well known in those days as a much-loved singer. People used to call him a rock god, and everywhere he went he was followed by an entourage of groupies. Women constantly threw themselves at him. He became used to so much attention, and soon became addicted to sex, drugs, and rock and roll. He knew nothing about real love, even though his beautiful songs claimed otherwise.

At his concerts, I would just stand back and watch as he worked the crowd, which was usually spellbound, especially the women who screamed out his name as he gyrated seductively around the stage. He was a remarkable singer, a natural tenor with an amazing vocal range, and he had the capacity to light up a whole room like electricity. I loved his creative talents and was convinced he must have channelled most of his songs as his whole body shook when he sang. His voice was a gift, so beautiful, raw and spiritual. The other members of the band were jealous of all the attention, of course, and constantly made crude jokes about him behind his back.

Things changed one day when Erik met a mysterious woman from England. Her name was Sara, and from the moment they met he was infatuated with her. The other members of the band were convinced she had bewitched him in some way because of the way he changed. He no longer seemed to have any interest in or control over anything, including his music.

One day Erik dropped into our house unexpectedly, looking for me. I hadn't seen him for ages, but I could see he wasn't his usual self. Keeping his head low and avoiding eye contact, he said in a strained, soft voice that he needed to talk. He wanted my advice about something confusing in his life. When I asked what it was, he said he was worried about Sara, his new girlfriend.

At first it had been fun, as Sara fitted right in with his friends in the band, and that was important to him as his music was his whole life. But suddenly everything changed. She became angry when he said he wanted to play in the band, and it was obvious that all she wanted was to have him to herself. Her interests involved reading occult books, playing with cards, chanting constantly, and making potions that she used in her healing practice, all of which was boring for him.

He said he was confused and didn't want to lose her, but it seemed ridiculous to me that this girl had such a hold over him.

'Look, I know it sounds crazy,' he said painfully, 'but you have to believe me. Sara has a cauldron and makes spells for her clients. Please don't say anything, especially to the others, but the whole thing's really weird and I need to work it out.'

Finally, he relaxed and pulled himself together. He took a deep breath and said he had discovered a strange object wrapped in coloured string tucked inside one of his boots when he went to clean them. He knew Sara must have put it there.

When he handed me the object, I said I would burn it and reassured him that everything would be okay. Then, with his permission, I gave him a spiritual healing. I placed lots of light in his aura, which was constricted and close to his body, and cleared away all the dark and negative energy that was around his head and affecting him so badly.

Erik soon settled down, and before long he was working hard again with the band.

Not long after this, I bumped into Sara at the bookstore in town. I'd had a feeling that would happen sooner or later. I'd sensed her energy around me, and seen flashes of a strange woman in my mind's eye after the healing I did for Erik.

As soon as she saw me, Sara marched towards me. She introduced herself, saying she'd heard so much about me and had been dying to meet me. Smiling sweetly, and constantly giving me hugs, she kept saying that she'd wanted us to be good friends for so long. She believed it was our destiny.

Sara was beautiful, with long black hair, and she looked like a tiny doll. But when I looked into her pale blue eyes, they were ice cold, totally empty and lacking any empathy or compassion, which made me shiver. Doubling my protection energetically, I remained calm and guarded my thoughts so she couldn't pick up on what I was thinking. My early training as a psychic medium came in handy, because every time she tried to read my mind, I blocked her psychic tentacles and invasive energy by humming in my head.

The next time I saw her, she asked me to come for lunch at her home, which was an hour's drive from town. She lived alone, as her parents had gone back to England and she had stayed to finish her studies. I didn't want to at first, but I did want to know more about her and what she was really up to.

When I arrived and stepped into her space, I could feel she was very lonely. Cluttered with books of an esoteric nature, it wasn't a happy place. I could see that she was heavily into the occult, as Erik had said, but on the darker side.

When I asked her about this, she became agitated and evasive, and refused to talk about it. Then, apparently changing her mind, she started talking proudly about how she used spells on a daily basis for everything in her life. If they didn't work, she would look into other things that went deeper.

Feeling uncomfortable, I began to wonder what she meant by that. She boasted, naively I thought, about how she now loved working with what she called 'darker energy' because it was stronger, more powerful and worked faster.

I told her it was obvious that she was out of her depth. She had no idea what she was doing and had been seduced by the delusional power the occult gave her. I said that the ramifications of working with dark energy and the occult had clouded her judgement. She had isolated herself and was clearly a very confused person.

The way she had manipulated poor Erik into submission like a puppet was totally disgusting, I told her.

I had no doubt that her meddling with powers far greater than her understanding would have its own ramifications. She would have to pay back karma; all actions have consequences at some point in the future.

After that day, I cut the energetic ties with her, protected myself and then helped Erik do the same. It seemed to work straightaway. Sara soon moved back to England to live with her parents. I prayed to spirit that she would receive help, as she had truly lost her way.

Moving on from Toxic Relationships

Always trust your feelings and honour what you know to be real, as trusting and tuning into your feelings and emotions is the key to connecting to your higher self, or the super-consciousness that is limited wisdom. It is also never wrong.

Learn to know your own limits for what feels right and what doesn't. Have the confidence to speak up and be heard. *No* is a powerful word. It's better to speak your peace than feel bad and drained by being taken advantage of.

Never allow people to control you, and nor should you allow yourself to think you owe them something. This will just make you feel guilty, which is a destructive emotion and dis-empowering. Remember, healthy boundaries are a sign of self-respect and self-love.

If you're having problems with boundaries, you could join a group of like-minded people who share your interests. Or you could seek counselling and other ways of supporting yourself and your wellbeing. You could keep a diary, which will give you a record of how far you've come. When you read it later, you'll see how your life has changed and how confident you've become. Maintaining boundaries is an art, but it's very easy to learn. Once you learn to say no, the rest is easy.

The following meditation exercise is good for releasing and clearing old energy patterns and spiritual contracts with people that are no longer useful, not just for you but also for the other person. It's positive and not harmful in any way, and it helps both parties move on. This exercise will help bring closure, and provide the energy and confidence needed for you to move on. There are no layers and it works extremely well.

MEDITATION FOR CUTTING OFF OLD ENERGIES

1. Find a quiet place in nature, or a sacred place, where you won't be disturbed for the duration of the meditation.

2. Light a white candle and place it on the altar.

3. Holding a photograph, or visualising the person you wish to cut ties with, visualise a blue figure of eight with gold in the middle. Visualise yourself on one side and the person you wish to cut ties with on the other side.

4. Now imagine cutting old ropes or vines that are wrapped around you, connecting you to the other person. Note what these ropes look like. What colour is the energy within the ties or ropes? Is this energy thick or thin? How does this energy make you feel?

5. Now imagine yourself with some oversized scissors, or a sword or knife. Whatever it is, make it big and cartoony to give it visual power. Using the implement, begin cutting through the ties connecting you to the other person.

6. When you have done this, cut out the centre of the figure of eight and blow the person away into a big pink bubble of love. This is your healing bubble, or healing room. No harm can come to anyone, as it is a sacred place of love.

7. As they float away, explain to them why it's not beneficial to have them tied to you. This is not about focusing on the person's negative traits but on releasing yourself from any negative effects they may have on you.

8. When you've done this, tell them who you are as a person and how you want to be treated in all your personal relationships.

9. Once you feel satisfied that you've communicated everything you need to, tell them you love them and forgive them, but the contract you once had is now terminated.

10. With love and blessings, say goodbye and step out of the healing bubble, sending the bubble full of green healing light into the source of love.

11. Close down all your chakras, or energy centres.

In this next meditation, you will be speaking directly to the person's higher self. It may take a while with difficult situations, and you may have to do it a couple of times before the other person is ready to give you any dialogue, but remember, with persistence miracles do happen. This is a great way to clear communication for all types of issues, including work, love and friendships.

Keep doing it until you get an answer. You're working with the person's higher self, and with patience and good intentions you will get results. I've used it on many occasions and it has often worked. When it hasn't, I simply send love and move on.

MEDITATION FOR TALKING TO THE HIGHER SELF

1. Find a quiet place where you can be alone for a while. Light a white candle and place it on the altar.

2. When you're ready, gently close your eyes and breathe deeply in and out three times, releasing any stress or negative emotion from your mind and body. As you relax, you will gradually feel all the tension leaving your body.

3. You will begin to feel lighter and more at ease as you drift deeper and deeper into relaxation.

4. When you're ready, in your mind's eye visualise a beautiful pure, pink bubble of forgiveness. Once you've done this, put yourself inside the bubble, and then the person you're having problems with.

5. Now begin a dialogue with them by telling them you're sorry and ask for their forgiveness. Tell them you want to move on and don't wish them any harm. Wait for a response. If they don't say anything, repeat what you've just said. Now ask them gently to forgive you.

6. When they've listened to what you have to say, ask them if they would like to say something as well. After you get a response, tell them that you now release all negative energy and the contract between you is finished. Then, with their permission, send them healing and love. If they say no, don't send it.

7. When you've finished, step out of the bubble and fill it with a beautiful green energy of light. Now send the bubble to the light for healing and transmutation. Once this has been done, open your eyes. Surrendering your problems to a higher source is the best way to bring positive outcomes.

8. Now close down all your chakras and energy.

If you're feeling scattered, blocked, confused, unable to move on, or all over the place, and you are finding it difficult to make decisions, try this next easy meditation.

Clearing the Old Energy

When I speak to clients about moving on from toxic relationships, I always suggest they either smoke any items related to the relationship, or throw them away to avoid psychic attack from the residual energy of the person they are no longer with. Energetically, it's all about using common sense to help you move on. Once you do this, you can create real magic in your life and you'll no longer feel stuck. Things will stop going wrong for no apparent reason, and you can begin to make changes in your life you have only dreamt about, including having better relationships.

Another good tip is to write down the person's name on a piece of paper and burn it in a small bowl. Fire transmutes energy and emotional turmoil, and it will help you embrace the renewal of the present without causing any harm to anyone. The experience is just that—an experience—and an example of a spiritual contract with that person who no longer needs any energy. Once this process is done, bury the ash in the garden and ask the nature spirits and angels to lovingly move it on.

Clearing the Clutter

When you're feeling stuck and are not moving on in your life, another practical thing to do is to clear the clutter. Most of us are great collectors of things we don't really need.

Prosperity	Fame	Relationships
Family & Health	Tai Chi	Creative, Children & Projects
Inner Knowledge & Intuition	Career	Helpful People & Travel

FRONT DOOR

You can begin with dividing up the different areas of your home into a 3 x 3 grid making nine equal sections, like a bagua map (above). Imagine you are standing at the front door, looking into your home. In the back right of the home there is the Relationship section. In the back middle is the Fame section, and in the back left is Prosperity. In front of the Prosperity section (middle left) is Family and Health. To the right of that, in the middle section of the home, is Tai Chi. In the middle right is the Creative, Children and Projects section.

Moving forward to the front of the home, on the front left side is Inner Knowledge and Intuition. Career is in the middle front, and to the front right is Helpful People and Travel.

By placing cures intuitively in each section, you can enhance the natural chi energy. Some of these cures include windchimes, coloured ribbons, lucky buddhas, mirrors, crystals, fresh flowers, plants, colours, water features, fountains, fish tanks and music. It's up to you to decide, as your intention is to bring more peace and harmony into your life. For example, if you live in cul-de-sac or near an intersection, a simple cure is to place a windchime at the front of the house to stop interfering energy.

To reduce the impact of aggressive neighbours, I love to place a mirror on an outside wall, which sends negative energy straight back. Bagua mirrors are good for this and can be bought quite easily over the internet.

Pallas Athena

Pallas Athena is the ancient Greek warrior goddess associated with freedom, truth, wisdom, fertility, the arts, warfare and handicraft. She is also known as Aletheia, the Roman goddess of truth. Her home is on Mount Olympus. Her temples, where she is worshipped, are at the top of the Acropolis in the central part of Athens, and the Parthenon is dedicated to her. She is regarded as the patron or protector of Athens and other Greek cities. She is shown wearing a helmet and holding a spear. Her symbols include owls, trees, snakes and the gorgoneion, a wooden panel or special amulet showing the Gorgon head, intended to guard against unwelcome guests. Zeus is known to wear this as well.

In Greek mythology, Pallas Athena was believed to have been born from the head of her father, and to have created the first olive tree. Athena was one of the three goddesses, including Aphrodite and Hera, whose feud resulted in the Trojan War, and she transformed Medusa into a Gorgon after she was raped by Poseidon in her temple. Draw on her energy when needed.

When you call on Athena's powerful energy it will help you move away from any toxic situations that no longer serve you, may be causing you harm, or bringing negativity, drama or sadness into your life. If you're not being heard no matter what you say or do, it's time to end the spiritual contract. If your energy is being wasted on a useless situation, often associated with senseless ego, nobody is a winner so it's time to walk away. It's time to focus on the positive and leave the past behind.

Setting up boundaries in life is an integral part of your development as a soul. When someone—a work colleague, boss, friend, family member, spouse or neighbour—ignores those boundaries by behaving in a way that makes you feel uncomfortable, compromised or stressed, it's up to you to respond in the correct way. Never be afraid to say no in any situation you find yourself in that does not serve you, or when you feel you're being compromised. Have the courage to walk away from toxic people, offensive behaviour and people who do not have your best interests at heart.

PREPARE YOUR ALTAR FOR PALLAS ATHENA

1. Light a white candle in your sacred space. Place some sweet-smelling or white flowers such as hybrid peony or lilies in honour of the goddess.

2. On the altar, place a symbol of a dove for peace, clear-quartz terminator for strength, a cluster of quartz for protection, and a red jasper crystal to help you with courage. (I love the smell of bergamot, grapefruit, violet and rose when working with this energy.)

3. Sit in a comfortable position and breathe in and out gently three times—in and out, in and out, in and out—until you feel relaxed.

4. When you are relaxed, repeat out loud three times: 'I call on the great, the bold and the wise wisdom of Pallas Athena to help give me the courage to move forwards with my life, with dignity, respect and love. I ask for your infinite courage to help me make the right choices in love.'

5. When you've finished, close down your energy and thank the goddess for working with you today.

32

SPIRITUAL TEACHERS

In general, a spiritual teacher is a person who guides, instructs or helps another in the process of gaining knowledge, understanding and skills. The goal of a spiritual teacher, or mentor, is unique in that the aim is not to transmit knowledge or understanding as much as it is to somehow bring about a recognition in the student of their own pre-existing nature. So spiritual teachers or mentors may teach a lot, or they may not teach anything, depending on what the student needs in that moment to experience this deeper recognition of their own true nature.

I've had many spiritual lessons in my life and will probably continue to do so. Not all spiritual teachers are good, but there can be a lesson to learn from the 'bad' ones. This is because, believe it or not, there are a lot of people in the world who are only out for themselves, and have no interest in you when it's your turn to be happy and successful. This is due to their own low sense of self-worth, pride, lust, envy, greed, ego and jealousy, and the high expectations they have for themselves without putting in any real work. This happens a lot in many industries, not just my own.

Spiritual teachers come in all shapes and sizes, and they can often be hard to detect. They may be people you least expect, such as family members, teachers, work colleagues, best friends, and people who you believe love you and you think you can trust. Unfortunately, you might discover that in reality they are attention seekers, or just want to ride on your coattails for money and power. The reality is that once these people have your attention and are tuned into you, they will go to great lengths to take everything they can.

After the experience, you will often feel foolish and sad because you didn't listen to your intuition or see the signs. Don't be too hard on yourself, though. These energies can very hard to detect, and people's intentions can be cleverly disguised. Once you have learned the lesson, it's time to let go. Just cut the ties and move on to people who are more on your own vibration.

You may sense, on meeting someone and feeling these energies, that you have a strong and sometimes loving connection, as if perhaps you have known each other before. As mentioned, these energies can be difficult to recognise as they come in all forms. They might have a strong position as trusted teacher, friend, lover, best friend, family member, employer, mentor or religious person. Many of these people, such as employers or mentors, should know better because of their position.

Things will start to go wrong over time, as this person may compete with you, or betray you for no apparent reason. The trouble is, you'll never know it's coming, even though others may try to warn you.

In a strange way, you appear as a threat to these people, and make them question the way they see themselves in the world. Often, and very sadly, you will learn that they are not who they say they are as they rip you off in any way they can. They can be good at manipulating you, perhaps by constantly telling you what you want to hear. Or they will outright lie and make up stories.

No matter what you do for these people, you will never receive reciprocating energy from them as they have no intention of helping you. Instead, they will help themselves to your hard-earned resources, time and energy, and speak negatively about you, with no integrity, to whoever will listen. Often the hurt will stay with you for a long time, thinking they will come back or in some way redeem themselves.

These types always come with powerful lessons that will help with the growth of your soul. The sooner you learn those spiritual lessons, the faster you will move on to better and happier realities.

33

SUPERSTITIONS, CURSES AND NEGATIVE ENERGY

Spiritual growth also means learning about negative energy in the shape of curses and psychic attack, both of which exist in our world. A lot of people are divided about whether curses, negative energy and psychic attack are real. Many people, from all types of cultures, are superstitious to a degree.

Growing up in a multicultural area, with people from all over the world, and having a busy practice as a healer and medium, I have seen and experienced many strange and interesting types of energies and phenomena, so I know that anything is possible.

For example, in the southern part of Europe, the *malocchio*, which is a curse, is believed to be protected by the Italian horn, which wards off bad energy. If not repelled, it can lead to misery, misfortune and sometimes illness. There is also the 'evil eye', which is a malevolent glare, usually inspired by hatred, jealousy and envy. Symbols of an eye are used for protection in many cultures, including Turkish and Slavic. When placed at the front of a house, they are effective in protecting against negative energy.

Many people from different backgrounds carry pictures or small statues of icons when travelling on planes as they make them feel safe, or they will sneak a good-luck charm into your hospital bag when you're having a procedure.

I believe there's always a balance between the light and dark forces in our world. All of these customs, and the words 'faith' and 'hope', give people the courage to deal with what life throws their way; they offer a feeling of security during difficult times.

As an energy worker and medium, I've heard other psychics say there's no such thing as curses. I wish it was true, but I beg to differ as I've experienced this phenomenon firsthand; I was cursed myself when I was younger.

Psychic Attack

Psychic attack is very real and can be a problem; as I have said and will continue to say, not everyone is light and love in the world. This includes lower-type lost spirits.

Psychic attack comes through people's negative thoughtforms and ill intentions. You'll always know when this is happening because you'll feel unwell, everything good in your life will disappear, you'll have nightmares and you'll suffer from unexplainable anxiety, and in some cases headaches. Some people complain about feeling knives in their back.

If the attack is being caused by an earthbound spirit, or lower-entity type, it can help when the spirit is rescued or moved on by a trained medium. On the other hand, it can be caused by a person, or group of people, sending negative energy. Today I tell clients to protect themselves with white light at all times, and to also imagine a blue cloak that covers the whole body, with a mirror ball to send the energy back so the person can receive the karma and learn the lesson.

Another way to stop any psychic attack or negative connection with toxic people is to either throw away any old items or gifts, or sweep them with sage, which will break the psychic link between you.

Amelia

Amelia was a lovely divorced woman in her sixties. After two knee replacements she was sent off to do physiotherapy and water therapy with a small group of other patients who had had the same operation.

It was a challenging time for Amelia, as one of the men took a fancy to her and kept asking her out, even though he said he was married. In the beginning they were texting in a friendly manner and she found his attention quite attractive, until his pursuit stepped up and he wanted a friends-with-benefits relationship. This horrified Amelia. She told him she wasn't interested in a relationship with him at all, or even a so-called friendship, for that matter.

Unfortunately, not taking no for an answer, he began to project sexual energy towards her through the astral in the evenings when she was in bed or even asleep. It became too difficult for Amelia to handle over time; she found it disgusting and not romantic at all. Finally, thinking she was going mad, she realised he was using her number on his phone as a link to 'psychically attack' her.

After connecting with me, I told her to delete his text and block him on social media. After cutting the ties, I suggested smoking out her home, especially the bedroom. This seemed to work immediately and she never heard from him again.

Meera

Meera was an Indian woman I first met when clearing her property with spirit rescue. She was a very successful businesswoman, and also spiritual, with a prayer room in her house. I saw Meera several times throughout the years, and she often spoke very fondly about her experience with a healer man from her temple, who at first appeared to be friendly and humble. She said he was very gifted, and she was happy to call him her guru. He never charged any money, and did many free healings for members of her family and friends. But being a generous person, she always offered him gifts for his services.

As time went on, she noticed a significant change in his ways and personality. One day, while visiting the temple, she got a shock when she saw him chatting merrily to a group of men while sticking needles into the spine of what looked like some type of small doll. After the men had finished talking, he threw the doll into a bin and left with his entourage.

On closer inspection, and not believing her eyes, she saw that the doll had human hair and an item of female underwear on its body. Trembling with fear, she decided to break away from the healer, blocking his number and disconnecting herself from the temple she had attended for many years.

Not long after this, she began to have nightmares. These nightmares became worse, intensifying until she couldn't sleep at all. She kept thinking she could see disfigured giants or demons surrounding her bed, and she was convinced that a dark type of energy had moved into her house. This negative energy was causing unnecessary unrest and constant arguments between her family members. In the end, her job suffered as well, as she was unable to concentrate, and before long she was without work.

In the meantime, the horrible man kept delivering messages to her home, asking her to come back to the temple.

When she finally rang me in tears, I told her to clear the home of anything he had given her in the past, and to give the home a good smoking using sage. This worked for a while, but before too long the energy had returned. When she told me this, I tuned into the home and saw, very clearly, a large nail above her doorway. I was convinced that this was this man's way of psychically attacking her. After investigating, she was shocked to find a weird copper nail drilled into the house above her front door. She had never seen it before, and when she tried to pull it out it was impossible to move. She called in a builder, who said he had never seen that type of nail before and wondered what it was. As soon as it was removed, she smoked out the home again and within days everything settled down, and she even got a new job.

Weeks later, she got confirmation on her community grapevine of what the man had been up to. He was discovered to be sending negative energy to everyone he knew, not just her, and when people stopped donating money, he sent dark energy to them. As a result, many innocent victims ended up in hospital, or even dead.

Things were fine for a quite a long time, and then she heard the news that he had died. All the unrest began once more. She started to smell the familiar musty cigarette smoke again, which made her believe his spirit had come back and was tormenting her.

When I tuned into the energy remotely over the phone, I saw a small spirit man standing at her front door. After I described him in great detail, she said, horrified and crying, that it sounded like he had returned again, but in spirit form this time. She kept saying she was convinced he wanted to manifest his evil energy into her, and take her down for standing up to him. Telling her not to worry, I called in my spirit team and we sent him off, never to return again.

Serena

Serena, a client of mine, was in a terrible marriage, which included domestic violence. Even when she finally left her husband, not only did she have nightmares, but she also thought about him all the time, making her feel anxious and fearful, as if she was still in the marriage. When I asked her if she'd kept any items from him, she said yes, telling me how she'd stored all the jewellery and other gifts under her bed.

When I explained that this was a direct psychic link to him that enabled him to keep attacking her, she was disgusted. She promised me she would sell most of it, and smoke out items she wanted to keep.

Not long after this, she phoned and said the energy had totally shifted and she was back to her old self again.

A good thing to be mindful of is that whenever you have negative people around you, or have toxic people in your home, they will always leave a psychic imprint, so don't hesitate to smoke out your home. It will work wonders. You can also place an energy grid around your property by imagining white light all around, and a blue cloak, just like you can do with your own person.

Toxic Energy

David was a client of mine who felt that he was being attacked when he joined a new company. He was very good at his work, but he felt there were a few people in his office who were jealous of his abilities. Suddenly he began to get headaches on a daily basis. He had never suffered from headaches before, and his doctor was baffled as to how to help him.

Headaches go hand in hand with negative energy or psychic attacks. They can also be caused by many other factors, anatomical, emotional and spiritual. This exercise using spiritual healing to treat headaches is an easy technique I learnt in my early training days with spiritual healing. It will help relieve tension in the head and neck area.

TECHNIQUE FOR EASING HEADACHES

1. Ask your client to sit on a chair and then stand behind them. Visualise white light running over yourself and your client.

2. Once you've activated your hand chakras by rubbing your hands together, begin to rake the aura with your hands, like you're clearing it of any negative energy.

3. Now, moving to the front of the person, move your hands to the top chakra, the crown, which is just above the top of your client's head. Placing your hands together, imagine spreading out the chakra a few times.

4. Now repeat this procedure with the third eye, which is in the brow area. Then go the throat and do the same.

5. When you've finished, channel, or visualise with your eyes, soft blue light around the whole area, as this will calm the area down. Over time, this will allow the chakras in the area to absorb the energy at their own pace and realign the energy.

6. When you've finished, close down.

MEDITATION FOR WHITE-ROOM TECHNIQUE

1. Find a quiet place where you won't be disturbed, or go to your sacred space and light a candle.

2. Sitting up straight and comfortable, slowly breathe in and out deeply three times to release any blocked energy.

3. Now gently visualise yourself starting to bring healing energy up from the earth star into your base chakra. As you do this, feel it moving around your body. Begin to blow out any negative energy through your mouth with your breathing.

4. Continue this process, moving slowly upwards, making sure you continue to breathe out, releasing as you continue up through all your chakras: begin with base (red), sacral (orange), solar plexus (yellow), heart (green), throat (blue), third eye (indigo), crown (purple), and transpersonal point (white). As you do this, feel all your chakras in gentle alignment.

5. Now imagine yourself in a white room. As you do this, with your eyes closed, look to the left and see if you sense anything there. If so, ask it to leave and go into the light, or wherever it came from.

6. Now check your right side and do the same until that is clear as well.

7. Repeat with the back and front. Do this until there's nothing in the white room with you. The white room, which is your auric, needs to be clear, with no attachments or clutter.

8. Now expand your energy to the size of the room. Then expand your energy field to the town or city you live in, and then finally out to the world. When you have done this, know that you are one with everything in the universe.

9. Now ask for all your soul energy that has been taken from you to come back. Ask with confidence that all negative energy, all negative curses, negative karma to be transmuted and returned to where it came from. Once you've done this, pull your energy back close to your body and feel your awareness in your heart.

10. Now gently wrap yourself like a beautiful cocoon of light with white light, then purple light, following with a sheaf of golden energy that washes all over you.

11. Once you've done this, use a blue cloak for protection whenever you feel negative energy around you, and a mirror ball to send energy back so the person sending the energy will receive the karma and learn the lesson. Finally, once you're ready to come back, feel all your energy return to your heart chakras, close down your energy, and open your eyes.

The following exercise is a clearing ritual to do in conjunction with the white-room exercise. Using both together works well.

RELEASING NEGATIVE ENERGY AND CURSES

1. Mix crushed garlic and grandfather sage together in a quarter of a bottle of pure olive oil. Then place a dab above the client's third eye, and on both wrists.

2. Light a white candle and, standing behind the client, place both hands on their shoulders. Call on great spirit to remove any negative energy, negative curses, outworn contracts, or any unwanted attachments to leave the client's energy field at once, and go into the light or back to the earth for healing for transmutation. Repeat this three times.

3. Once you've done this ritual you'll feel a very subtle energy shift, or lightness, in your client. Negative thought forms, earthbound energies and souls are all treated with the white light and sent into the light, or back to where they came from. In some cases, I send dark energy into the earth for healing. Simply burning sage or smoking a house will work wonders, as it weakens the negative energy, and I generally ask the client to do this.

4. At the end of the session, ask the client to write down the person's name on a piece of paper and burn it. Once they've done this, they should bury the ashes in the garden and trust the earth elementals to take care of the situation. Always trust your own judgement when working with good healers, because sometimes people cannot do what they say they can.

People ask me if this procedure is safe. As mediums work always with good intentions, it does not hurt anyone, unlike putting hateful curses on people, or throwing out negative thoughts to harm someone. It's simply creating time out by putting everybody's emotions and negative thoughts on hold.

Maria

Maria, a client, got taken down badly by a relative who had paid a woman who worked with the dark forces for a curse. Maria's whole life was turned upside down. She got really sick with a heart condition, which was ridiculous as she was a health fanatic; the family lost their life savings in the stock exchange; good friends simply disappeared; and her daughter was in a terrible accident, losing one of her legs. Within a period of two years, Maria's whole life spun out of control right in front of her eyes.

Finally, she came to me, totally saddened and desperate for answers. Sometimes you have to fight fire with fire. The dark energy around her was incredible to see psychically; I could sense the evil dark energy and hatred wrapped around my client. When I told her this, she said she understood. She knew exactly when it happened and who had done this.

The first thing I did was the cut-the-ties exercise between Maria and the offending person who was sending all the negative and destructive energy. Once this was done, I used the white-room technique to clear the dark energy.

When this was done, she sat up and said she felt suddenly lighter in her body, which was overwhelming, as she had felt so heavy and trapped for so long.

Then I told her to wrap a white light around her for protection, and a blue cloak, and use a mirror ball. The mirror would send the negative energy back to the person so they could learn the karmic lesson. She was to do this every day on awakening until she felt better. She could also use it as a healing practice every day to shield and protect her energies from harsh energies. Like everyone, Maria lived in a busy world that is often in turmoil.

Next, I asked her to write the person's name on a piece of paper, then place it in the freezer for forty-eight hours. Then she was to burn the paper and bury the ashes in the garden; with good intentions, the nature spirits would heal all negative energies between the two people.

The good thing was, no harm would come to anyone involved and a healing would take place for both parties, with no residual negative energy, or bad karma, left behind in the past, present and future.

Within two days Maria rang me and said she had had a dream about the offending person, the woman's family, and the witch who had sent the curse. In the dream, at first she'd been frightened but then she'd suddenly heard what sounded like a loud scream. Finally, they had all turned their backs on her and walked away. She didn't know what to think and was terrified. I told her it was a good omen as the spell, or negative energy, had been broken and the people would not be returning. I suggested she give her bedroom a good smoke out with some sage to get rid of the negative energy in the room, and then open the windows to allow the new energy, or chi, to come in.

34

RAISING YOUR VIBRATION

Allow yourself to be aware of your thought forms. Be careful what you wish for, because you might just create it. Everything you think, say or feel becomes your reality. Think how easy it is to put yourself down. We all do it, and we all carry old programs we've had since we were little.

Sometimes we forget about the negative monkey chatter in our heads, but it often seems to take over and sabotage a lot of things for us, no matter how hard we try to change. How many times do you hear people say that they always seem to be walking up a mountainside and nothing changes, no matter what they do on a conscious level? For example, if you keep saying you're stupid or fat, people will look at you like that.

We also need to be aware of our negative thoughts to and about other people who have caused us harm, as this can cause psychic attack, which is not a good outcome for anybody involved.

The first step is positive thinking: never let another negative thought about yourself enter your head. Taking personal responsibility is a big step. The power of positive thinking is an incredible force as it affects everything that's going on in your life. If you take the time to think about it, we are the creators of our own destiny, as we are all made up of energy and are natural transmitters that draw our experiences to us.

The golden rule is to take personal responsibility and change the energy and patterns you constantly draw in your life. You are made up of, and carry, so many emotions, all of which affect everything that happens to you in your life. Energy is designed to flow in and out like your breath, but sometimes it can get stuck.

The law of attraction is based on the concept that like attracts like, that positive energy attracts positive energy. If you can train your mind to think positive thoughts you will attract more positive energy into your life.

Positive thinking takes practice. Start by observing your own self-talk, and be aware of what you say to people and how you think. If it's negative, replace it with something positive. Affirmations are good for this. As you go about your day, be aware of your thoughts and attitude. If you catch yourself thinking something negative, sweep it away and replace it with something positive.

Positive thinking is not about ignoring the more challenging aspects of life; it's about approaching all situations in a positive and productive way.

Powerful Affirmations

Affirmations can be used when you wake up, while exercising, in meditations and almost every part of your day. They can be used in any area of your life. As with exercise, you need to train your brain to believe that you are loved, respected and deserving, as whatever you believe and tell yourself is what you become in the world.

Affirmations are an incredible life tool to have, and you might be surprised to see how easy they are to use. Once you start to use them on a regular basis, you'll learn how much fun it is to play with the energy. You'll watch in wonderment how dramatically your life will change.

I call affirmations the secret to creating success; they are soul food, nurturing and vital for your spiritual growth and the progression of your super-conscious mind. Over time and with patience, and once you've raised your vibrations by being positive, you'll say goodbye to toxic relationships as you'll no longer be attracted to that energy. Instead, you'll attract only wonderful experiences instead of constant worries, toxic situations, repeated sad situations and constant bad luck that in the past have always knocked at your door.

Sometimes I turn affirmations into little songs, and sing them to the tune of favourite songs I know when I exercise. Some of my favourite affirmations:

- *Every day in every way, I am happy, safe and secure.*
- *I always attract loving, happy people who accept me for who I am.*
- *I deserve the best always, thank you.*
- *I always find myself in the right place at the right time to receive golden opportunities. Golden opportunities come to me always.*
- *I see joy and love in everything around me.*
- *I now forgive everyone and anything that has ever hurt me.*
- *I am always protected and safe with my angels and guides around me.*
- *I am always drawn to the right energy people that are on my wave length.*

- *I am eternally blessed and thank the God force or spirit for all the blessings I have in my life now.*

Soon these simple positive affirmations, which are powerful words, will without a doubt become a part of your belief system, and nobody can ever take them away from you because you own them.

Create a Gratitude List

Give thanks for everything you have in your life with a gratitude list. We often take things for granted, and have no real idea what we have accomplished or achieved in our lives. When you sit down and think about it, you'll be surprised how far you've come and, best of all, how well you've been able to move on and basically just get on with your life, no matter how hard the nightmare has been. Many people have had to start again with nothing, only to move forward, change their lives and live a life they have only dreamt about. With determination, a strong belief that you deserve the best always, and good thoughts, you can lift your vibration to a higher rate, and attract only good experiences and better outcomes.

Daily Meditation

Meditating for at least twenty minutes a day should be an integral part of your busy life. Without a doubt, it's an energy booster; it clears your mind and energy on every level. When you have the time to do this twice a day you'll be able to manifest a life of abundance, since good things will come to you when you put out into the universe what you want.

Meditation and visualisation go hand in hand when you want to draw opportunities or good things into your life. Instead of running around chasing opportunities, draw them in instead and watch as your desires come to you.

Make it a rule to close down all your energy chakras after you meditate or work with people energetically, or you can become scattered and ungrounded.

The Magic of Prayer

Always remember the gift of prayer, as it's a straight line of communication to the spirit world and the guides, angels, spirit helpers and loved ones who are connected to your love eternally. No matter what you may think or believe, you will always be assisted, and your prayers will be heard, no matter the odds. Don't forget to ask for things.

Regular Exercise

How good is exercise. Not only does it boost your mood, help with physical activity, improve your weight, give you more energy and years, and clear your head, but it will also improve your sex life and make you feel like a million dollars, ready to take on the world. There are just too many pluses to ignore. No matter what your current weight, being active will boost your high-density lipoprotein (HDL), or 'good' cholesterol, and decrease unhealthy triglycerides. This one-two punch keeps your blood flowing smoothly, which decreases your risk of cardiovascular diseases.

Psychic Protection

White energy, or the power of love itself, is the most powerful energy in the world and the universe, as it is universal unconditional love. By simply wrapping white light around your bed, yourself, children, pets, family and earthly possessions, you will always have protection. When I need extra protection, I always use purple and gold, like the sun, which I wrap around the light whenever I'm around toxic people or in difficult situations. Then I use a blue cloak and add a mirror ball for reflection so the negative energy that is thrown at me will return to the sender so they can receive the karma, because they will never learn the lesson otherwise.

Calming Baths

To calm yourself, have a bath with Epsom's salts, or sea salt, and add lavender. I call this my goddess ritual. This has the power to cleanse your aura and clear any bad energy that may be harmful. If you feel you've been cursed, attacked or are oversensitive, light some candles, draw a warm bath and soak your whole body in the warm water, even the back of your head. While you're having a nice long soak, think only of positive, kind and encouraging thoughts, imagining all the clutter of the day being washed away. When you step out of your soak, you will feel relaxed, energised and reborn.

Smoking Your Home, Space and Body

I mostly work remotely these days, so I will always, when doing any type of clearing or spirit rescue, tell the client to smoke out the house or property with some sage mixed with dried Australian gum leaves. Sometimes, if the energy is really toxic and heavy,

I will suggest doing this a couple of times, as it often works in layers. This will clear the negative energy. It's an old shamanistic practice passed down by the indigenous people.

Some people also believe mugwort, wormwood and vetiver are particularly powerful when it comes to warding off bad spirits, so you might want to carry some around with you. Fill up a small cloth sack with the herbs, and tie it around your waist or put it in your pocket.

35

HEALING WITH NATURE

Have you ever wondered why nature is so healing and beneficial for us all? It's because nature is full of nature spirits, or elementals—clear and powerful spirits and energies that live in the earth surrounding our world. Elementals are nature spirits, magical beings that have lived together peacefully since the beginning of time. These spirits include earth, wind, fire and air. Together, they work with the angelic kingdom to bring healing into our lives.

Earth Spirits

Earth spirits have a strong connection to the elements and are found in nature. These earth spirits are the pixies, gnomes, elves, leprechauns, trolls and goblins living freely in our forests, woods and mountains. They serve mankind at the psychical level, and tend the earth through the four seasons so living things are taken care of for their daily needs.

Of all the earth spirits, gnomes are known to be the most shy, gentle and humble. They love simplicity, and like to stay in their communities and not wander. Their clothes, for both male and female, are simple and unadorned, like their personalities. Female gnomes are taller than males, and mostly hairless.

Pixies are the most colourful of the earth spirits. They are fickle by nature, like to show off and adorn themselves with shiny sparkles, and wear oversized clothes, odd shoes and colourful hats. These delightful beings love to gossip and travel on the backs of caterpillars or ladybugs. They like to move around a lot and find it difficult to stay in one spot, unlike gnomes.

Goblins, on the other hand, are dull, very secretive, quite lazy and don't like mixing, tending to live away from other earth spirits. They are gentle creatures, but are known to succumb to temptation if it comes their way.

Elves are the worker bees of the kingdom, congregating in large groups in collectives, and have the gift, like wizards and magicians, of helping all humanity. They dedicate their lives to helping others and are known to be the healers of the forests.

All the earth spirits are known for purging the earth of toxins and pollutants that are dangerous to man, animals and birds—all creatures small and big on Earth.

Wind Spirits

Wind spirits, or sylphs, live harmoniously in the ether surrounding our world, and are known to not only inspire us but also to bring us new ideas, making way for creative energies and thoughts when we feel stuck in our lives. Sylphs tend and direct the flow of air currents and atmospheric conditions. They are also the bearers of sustaining prana, which nourishes all living things. Sylphs are known to draw their power from sunlight and that's why they're rarely seen at night.

The common crow has sylph energy; crows are known to symbolise magic in our world. Some say that sylphs' magical qualities include prophecy, skill and knowledge. Historically, the ancient Celts believed the crow to be an omen of death. They were said to be sorcerers and witches, and the crow's-foot symbol was used to cast death spells. This is far from the truth, as crows are highly amusing and very family orientated. Along with the owl family, crows are fascinating, highly intelligent and can be taught to communicate with humans.

Over the years I have had many crow families living near my place of work. Every time I decided to record any meditation sessions, I would always hear the crazy crows talking and squawking in the background, almost as if they were demanding their right to be included. Sometimes when I talk to other psychics on the phone, I'll hear a crow calling out in the background, as if it's giving me a sign that this person is working on the same vibration as me.

It is no surprise to me if I'm followed by a flock of crows when I'm clearing homes and properties because they are known for shamanistic healing, and make me feel as if they're helping me clear the negative energy.

Fire Spirits

Elemental fire spirits, or salamanders, are known as the spark of life within all things. It's said that they invoke power for the first step in every process. This provides the initial spark for all life, from the spark of conception of a baby to the spark of inspiration for new ideas and thoughts.

Every process begins with fire. It allows variation in a process so that activity can be appropriate to its time and place. Fire is the least dense of all elementals and stimulates air, working through the balance of gases in the atmosphere and bringing it to a state of activity so it can support life. It's also the opposite of water. Without the spark of fire, the salamander's life and matter begin to decay, corrode and disintegrate. With fire comes transition, change and new beginnings, where we welcome new realities with better outcomes.

Water Spirits

Water spirits are graceful undines, or water fairies: beautiful winged water beings that live near rocky pools, streams and rivers.

For years I used to take my students into the bush to teach them how to tune into flowers to make essences, and to see tiny little fairies around rocky water pools, waterways and rivers. It's easy to see them, because when you look carefully, especially above the water, you can often see tiny little lights, glistening and busily moving around and flickering in the sun. Nature orbs are different, as they are bigger and don't move around so much.

Water fairies dominate the element of water. They are interdimensional beings that are easy to channel, existing in a realm within the earth. They are quite regal and like to ride on the backs of birds or rabbits. They are here to serve, tend and nurture the earth. They work hand in hand with angels, but are connected to the earth, while the angels live in the heavens and visit.

There are also mermaids, beings that are swift and subtle in their movements, controlling the tides with the moon, connected to the oceans and other bodies of water on earth. They are also known as the shape-shifters of the elemental kingdom. Shape-shifters have the ability to change their physical form at will, and can be visualised as half human, half fish, able to assume any form. They are known to cleanse polluted waters, and their bodies are cosmic currents of spirit. They also help us with our emotional bodies and the subconscious worlds.

MEDITATING IN NATURE

1. Go to your sacred space in nature where you won't be disturbed, and imagine a column of vibrant white light washing down over you.

2. As you do this, feel this powerful light and energy filling your entire being. Now breathe deeply, feeling yourself going deeper and deeper, then anchoring your energy deep into mother earth, where you will connect with the source of the earth's pure energy of unconditional and bountiful love.

3. Now bring this energy back up to the base chakra. Feel it slowly traveling up through all your energy chakras, expanding everywhere, into the cells of your body, then feel it gently rise above your head, higher and higher, going further and further into the ether all around you, until you know you are one with everything in the multiverse.

4. Once you've done this, expand your energy and awareness all around you, pushing it out as far as you can to the edge of the forest or bushlands.

5. Now slowly feel all your senses opening up. Start with your feelings. What does nature feel like around you? Is it calm, healing and tranquil? If it's full of trauma and turmoil, send unconditional healing to everything around you and move on. Now go further, expanding your energy even more, enjoying the calmness and soothing energy all around you.

6. Now open up your senses to smell. Smell everything around you: the fresh smell of the lush grass, the forest trees, the moist ground, the sweet perfumes of the wild flowers. Find as many smells as you can.

7. Now listen to all the different sounds: the birds, the insects, the breeze in the trees and grasses around you. As you continue, feel the taste in your mouth. Is it bitter or sweet? What sensations are you now sensing?

8. Now, in your mind's eye, slowly scan the area around you and take notice of anything you can see. As you do this, feel the warm gentle caress of the sun on your body, as if it's giving you more energy for the day.

9. If you're having difficulty with your mind chatter you can use a mantra like 'So Hum': repeat those words in your mind's eye as you breathe slowly in and out, and this will help.

10. When you're ready to call in the elementals of nature, take a deep breath and summon the earth spirits to come closer: the wind spirits, water fairies and fire elementals. Imagine them sitting all around you in a circle and thank them for coming in today. As you do this, one by one imagine what they look like in your mind's eye. Take the time to do this slowly, and then ask them if there's a message for you that may help you and give you guidance in your life.

11. When you've finished, thank the elementals for coming in today and wish them love, gratitude and healing.

12. It's now time to close down and come back into your body. Do this by closing down all your energy centres, or chakras, by imagining them like tiny lights in your body winking out. Then imagine yourself anchoring all your energy back into the earth, being grounded, and once again back in your body.

13. Now open your eyes slowly and see the new day. Don't be surprised at how much calmer and more energised you feel. You've just had an interesting experience, so remember to write everything down and compare your notes to other days.

A Fairy Garden

This wonderful idea will bring good harmony, healing and energy to your home and family by creating a magical healing space with your own fairy garden. The intention is to create a healing space in your home with the benefits of nature and all it has to offer. The best position is the far left of your home, or backyard, as this is your prosperity area.

This is beneficial for everyone, and is especially helpful for people who live in busy cities as they often have very little free time and can never really access the healing benefits of nature. Fairy gardens are very playful energetically. Children love them, and they're very nurturing for the child within, as they open you up to the elemental world of nature.

Not only is a fairy garden mystical, but it's also decorative, the perfect place to visit when you're feeling down in the dumps.

It's also the ideal place for sick plants to recover, as the energy from the nature spirits is amazing, energising and so very healing.

If you don't have a garden and live in a unit or smaller space, you can create a fairy garden in a pot, which is just as effective and healing, working in the same way. You can have your pot near a window, filled with fresh plants and bits and pieces, perhaps a small fairy representing nature and the elements, or a gnome or playful butterfly. By creating a fairy pot, you will always attract positive energy from the elemental kingdom, which will be happy to look after your home and bring you not only good luck, but also harmonious energy.

If even non-believers look long enough, they might just see an air spirit, like a sylph, shaking a lonely leaf on a tree when there is no wind, or a light fairy buzzing around that might make them feel light-hearted.

CREATING A FAIRY GARDEN

1. You need to find the right spot for your fairy garden, and remember, you can use a large pot on your balcony if you're living in a unit.

2. The area you choose needs to be quiet and, if possible, near water. This could be a fish pond, water feature, bird bath or pool, as fairies or undines love to be near water.

3. In the surrounding potted trees or plants, if you have any, place wind chimes, as this is an invitation to the sylphs or air spirits, along with butterflies and birds.

4. Some people also like to create a space with little lights, which can look beautiful and charming, especially at night. Children love this.

Around my garden I have a few statues of fairies, unicorns, gnomes, devas and elves, and a little house and plaque welcoming everyone to feel free to visit the fairy garden whenever they feel down or need inspiration in their lives. When visitors or children come, I ask them to be quiet and respectful of the space as it's an invitation to another world.

Don't be surprised if your dogs or cats like to spend most of their time lounging around the area because, without a doubt, they will love the energy. It's also a good place to heal sick plants as, over time, they will improve as you will have created an energy vortex.

CONCLUSION

LIFE IS A STAGE

The spirit world, I have come to discover, is a vast consciousness of love and light and healing. To some people, it can seem like a place in nature, or a great city. The spirit world is just an arm's length away, but in another dimension.

It's a good thing to know that when you die there is no ending; rather, it's a transition to the spirit world, which is not only brighter and lighter than the world you have known, but also takes you to a higher consciousness. Once you arrive with your guide, you are taken to the life review and many other stops.

The greatest spiritual lesson I have learned in my life is that often the people you meet in life are not who they say they are. I've also learned that light-energy people will never blend with dark-energy people; they are poles apart and can never live in harmony. Negative, or dark-energy people, can exist within your own family. They can be your friends, lovers, work colleagues, and trusted people in the community.

I have come across many people in this industry who claim to be lightworkers but are actually the opposite. It can be confusing, because dark-energy people come in all kinds of disguises, shapes and sizes, and can be hard to detect.

Awareness is a valuable key, so always follow your intuition and gut feelings, as they are seldom wrong. A good friend of mine always used to say: 'The "but" in your gut is never wrong.' If a situation doesn't feel right, or a person feels toxic, trust your gut, as it's always right. Once you've learned to recognise this energy, my advice is to simply move on, let it go, and make a point of living in peace and harmony, as that is your birthright.

To love other people can be easy for some, but self-love can often be a different story for those who have experienced too many painful and difficult experiences on their journey in life.

As an eternal soul, you may be carrying this negative energy of low self-worth from your childhood or other lifetimes as unnecessary baggage. When you incarnate on Earth again, each lifetime you live has a theme, and once you have learnt the lesson or understood the experience you can move on to a higher frequency, with better realities and outcomes. By reconnecting to your soul, you will experience joy, peace and newfound freedom.

The work of a medium helps people reflect on the spirit of hope that life is eternal, the spirit of salvation, the spirit of strength, and the spirit of unconditional love in its highest form.

Your soul will live on forever, receiving survival evidence, or what is called proof of survival, and this is one of the best types of healing in the world. It helps you move on and understand that there is really no death, only new beginnings; it's like the end of one story and the beginning of a new chapter of another.

When you think about it, we live in an exciting and incredible world, with so many possibilities, outcomes and realities.

Love and blessings
Kerrie

RECOMMENDED READING

The Spiritual Awakening Process, Mateo Sol and Aletheia Luna, Amazon, 2019.
Crystals for Healing, Karen Frazier, Callisto Media, 2022.
The Third Eye, T Lobsang Rampa, Ballantine Books, 1956.
The Astral Projection Guidebook, Erin Pavlina, Amazon, 2013.
Healing Lost Souls in the Aura, William J Baldwin, Hampton Roads, 2003.
Between Life and Death, Dolores Cannon, Ozark Mountain Publishing, 2013
Journey of the Souls, Michael Newton, Llewellyn Worldwide Ltd, 1994.
Flower Therapy, Doreen Virtue and Robert Reeves, Hay House, 2012.
Vibrational Healing Through the Chakras, Joy Gardner, Crossing Press, 2006.
Auras and Colours, Paul Lambillion, Gateway, 2001.
Inside your Dreams, Rose Inserra, Rockpool Publishing, 2021.
Your Dream Interpreter, Tony Crisp, Cico Books, 2005.
Witnessing the Impossible: The Diary of the Scole Experiment, Robin Foy, Campion Books, 2023.
Explore Your Past Lives, Paul Roland, Godsfield Press, 2005.
Celebrity Oracle, Kerrie Erwin, Rockpool Publishing, November 2023.
Spirit Rescue, Kerrie Erwin, Llewellyn Publishing, April 2023.
Mediumship, Kerrie Erwin, Rockpool Publishing, 2021.
Clearing, Kerrie Erwin, Rockpool Publishing, 2020.
Sacred Signs, Kerrie Erwin, Rockpool Publishing, 2017.
Sacred Space, Kerrie Erwin, Feng Shui Rockpool Publishing, 2016.

Sacred Soul, Kerrie Erwin, Rockpool Publishing, 2015.
Learning to Work with the Tarot, Kerrie Erwin, Cards-Balboa, 2013.
Spirits Whispering in My Ear, Kerrie Erwin, White Feather Publishing, 2012.
Memoirs of a Suburban Medium, Kerrie Erwin, White Feather Publishing, 2011.
Magical Tales of the Forest, Kerrie Erwin, White Feather Publishing, 2010.

ABOUT THE AUTHOR

Kerrie Erwin

With a nursing, teaching, performing arts and musical background, Sydney-based international medium Kerrie Erwin has lived between two worlds since childhood and is able to see and hear spirit people talking.

Realising her true calling when she was very young, she now works professionally as an energy worker, with spiritual mediumship, trance, psychical mediumship and clairvoyance, focusing on spirit rescue, hauntings, and connecting people to loved ones that have passed over into the spirit world.

Kerrie has taught mediumship and metaphysics for many years, reads tarot cards, and works with Feng Shui.

She is also trained in spiritual hypnotherapies and past-life regression.

Kerrie is also a published author of 11 books, regularly writes for magazines as a freelance writer, and has worked on 2DayFM Sydney and various other radio and TV shows.

She also produces and delivers the The Kerrie Erwin spiritual show, a successful stage show she regularly tours around Australian clubs and other venues. She also has a free segment on social media at her Kerrie Erwin Public Facebook Page, giving free messages and spiritual advice to help the community.

CONTACT KERRIE

Kerrie Erwin
Spiritual medium, clairvoyant and author
www.facebook.com/KerrieErwinPublicFigure
www.instagram.com/mediumkerrieerwin
www.pureview.com.au

Manufactured by Amazon.ca
Acheson, AB